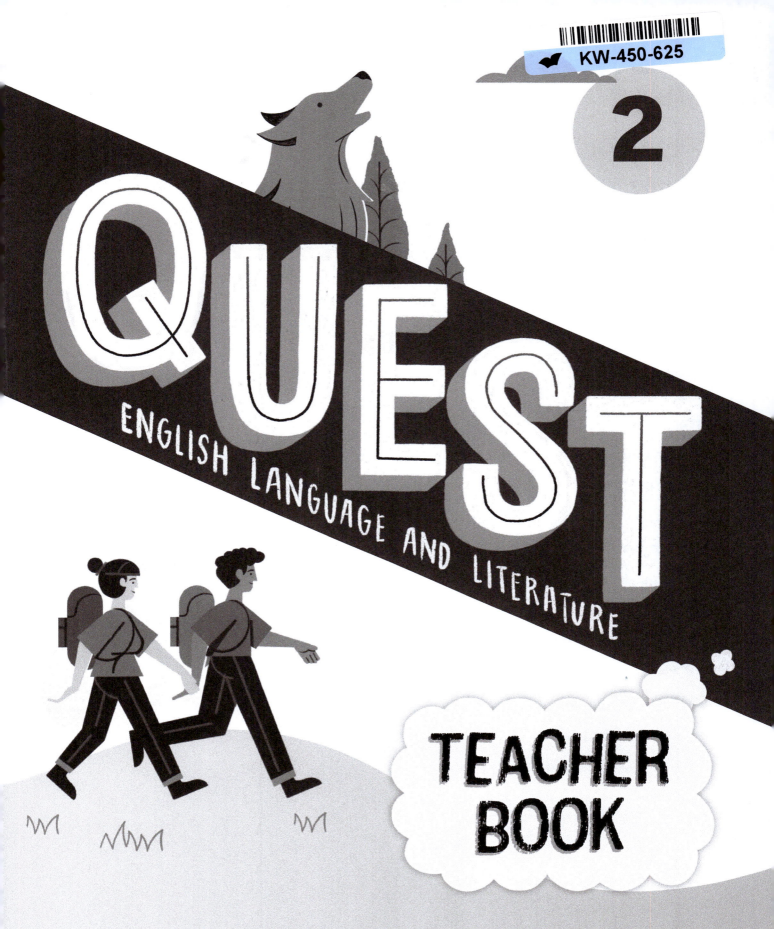

QUEST

ENGLISH LANGUAGE AND LITERATURE

2

TEACHER BOOK

Sarah Eggleton

Lance Hanson

OXFORD
UNIVERSITY PRESS

Contents

Welcome to Quest

Quest delivers the 11–14 segment of the *Oxford Smart* Curriculum Service for English and has been written to:

- build on the variety of learner experiences at KS2 and explore English as a unique discipline, empowering, engaging and motivating both learners and teachers
- support teachers in delivering a diverse, relevant and challenging curriculum, drawing on the varied and disparate identities and interests of KS3 students and validating their experiences and ideas
- look back across the rich literary heritage of English Literature but also forwards to a future dominated by the digital world
- provide access to high-quality texts from a wide range of writers, both classic and contemporary, and from a range of backgrounds, cultures and experiences
- offer flexibility and choice while still delivering the core skills and knowledge so that teachers can customise their route through the resources and choose from alternative source texts to best suit the needs of their students
- enable efficient and effective progress tracking, giving teachers the confidence that students will be ready to embark on their GCSE studies by the end of Year 9
- allow teachers to identify and address misconceptions and misunderstandings with low-stakes assessments plus intervention before moving on.

The *Oxford Smart* Curriculum Service

The *Oxford Smart* Curriculum Service for English is aligned to and develops the skills and knowledge essential for accessing the KS3 and KS4 National Curriculum for English. It is underpinned by six core curriculum pillars which connect content, pedagogy, assessment and data to deliver a coherent and responsive learning experience. The curriculum has been built on a strong foundation of pedagogical research and will generate its own evidence and impact from experts, educators and learners. Over time, this portfolio of evidence will inform and inspire future curriculum evaluation and development, supported by a programme of Continuing Professional Development (CPD).

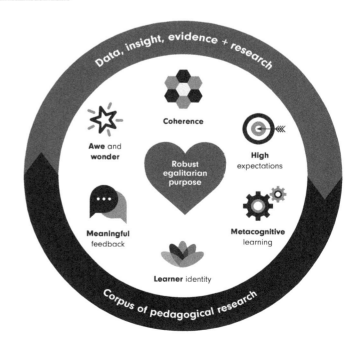

Quest and the six pillars

The six core curriculum pillars that underpin *Oxford Smart* English are as follows:

 Pillar 1: Provide clear and coherent curriculum pathways

Quest provides a coherent learning structure by using a broad range of texts and topics which build towards GCSE, providing links to key themes in the set texts and poetry. Chapter 1 *Texts all around us* in Student Book 1 lays the foundations for what students will encounter throughout the rest of the course, introducing key concepts linked to a range of genres and text types. The knowledge features in the Student Book ensure students understand what they are learning and the skills activities enable them to apply their knowledge. The alternative texts and activities in the worksheets on Kerboodle allow for choice within the curriculum pathway, while still delivering the core skills and knowledge.

 Pillar 2: Hold equally high expectations, aspirations and ambitions for all learners

Quest introduces students to challenging texts, topics and ideas in an accessible way through its thematic approach. It focuses on English as a discipline, building on learning from KS2 but focusing on what is different about English at KS3. The regular, low-stake quizzes at the end of each unit help teachers identify misconceptions and gaps in understanding, and the additional source texts in the worksheets on Kerboodle can be used for support or challenge.

 Pillar 3: Enable responsive teaching and learning that continually evolves and improves

Throughout Quest, skills and knowledge are revisited in fresh and different ways, and in different contexts, to help with intervention and to enable teachers to support students where needed. Activities build carefully and are scaffolded within each unit to help identify where students might need additional support. After each unit of work in the Student Book, students' knowledge will be tested through a mini-checkpoint quiz and next steps will be automatically generated to support or extend their learning. The units of work build to half-termly checkpoint assessments that allow students to apply their knowledge and put their skills into practice. Additional spelling, grammar and punctuation quizzes will also help to target misconceptions, gaps in learning and areas that need more explicit teaching.

 Pillar 4: Support engaged, self-regulated and metacognitive learning

Metacognitive strategies are embedded throughout the units of the Student Book to promote student independence and develop self-regulated learners, with guidance and ideas about additional overviews in the Teacher Book. The chapter openers will activate prior knowledge, while the learning overviews give students a clear pathway of what and how they will be learning and why. Additional information and support for embedding metacognition is provided as part of the CPD and Research Hub on Kerboodle.

 Pillar 5: Promote development of learner identity and identification with curriculum content

The topics in Quest have been carefully chosen for their relevance to students. The Student Books and Kerboodle resources include texts from contemporary and classic writers from a range of backgrounds, cultures and experiences. The alternative texts in the worksheets on Kerboodle allow teachers to tailor their lessons to a particular group of students. Activities throughout the resources encourage students to draw on their own contexts, knowledge and ideas to develop their reading, writing, speaking and listening identities.

 Pillar 6: Stimulate fascination, awe and wonder in discovery of self and the world around us

The units in Quest introduce students to engaging themes, big ideas and key concepts that will encourage and stimulate debate and engage learners. The source texts have been chosen in order to unlock new worlds and offer insights into alternative experiences and, along with the themes and topics covered, will help students to build their hinterland knowledge and discovery of self. There are also suggestions for class readers and further reading to help expand students' knowledge and boost their wider understanding of texts and the world around them.

 More information on each pillar can be found in the CPD and Research Hub on Kerboodle.

Overview of Quest

Quest comprises digital and printed Student Books and Teacher Books for each year of KS3, digital worksheets to support the Student Book, assessment resources, and research and professional development resources. The course aligns to the skills and knowledge set out in the National Curriculum for KS3 and is underpinned by the six pillars of the *Oxford Smart* Curriculum Service. Content is delivered through engaging topics, each of which explores 'big ideas' to help students understand what they need to learn and why, and to encourage and stimulate debate and ideas.

Students will cover nine topics, one per term. Topics and texts have been chosen because they are engaging, relevant and inspiring. They will also lay the foundations for the types of texts and themes that students will study at KS4, helping to prepare them for their GCSE course.

Each chapter has a theme and poses and answers key questions:

	1 Texts all around us	2 Crime and consequences	3 Journeys and discoveries
Year 7	• What is a text? • How have language and texts evolved over time? • Whose voices have been heard and how can you use your voice today?	• What lies behind readers' fascination with crime? • How has crime writing changed over time? • What makes a great detective?	• How have stories of journeys of discovery shaped English literature? • How is character revealed by the challenges and dangers faced? • Why do we undertake journeys? How can they help us to better understand ourselves?

	1 Power and influence	2 Terror and wonder	3 Wild places and urban landscapes
Year 8	• Do your decisions rely on your emotions or your intelligence? • How do writers appeal to a reader's emotions when they attempt to influence or persuade? • Who are the influencers – both now and in the past?	• How does fear fuel the imagination? • Are terror and wonder two sides of the same coin? • How has Gothic fiction shaped English literature over the past 250 years?	• How have different environments inspired writers' imaginations? • How have writers expressed ideas about the relationship between humans and their environment? • How do writers explore the spaces in between?

	1 Truth and reality	2 Utopia and dystopia	3 Youth and age
Year 9	• What is the news and what makes a good journalist? • How can we tell truth from lies? • How has the way news is gathered and distributed affected language use, presentation and objectivity?	• Can the perfect society ever exist? • Is one person's utopia another person's dystopia? • How have utopias and dystopias been depicted in fiction?	• Does age bring wisdom or do the young see the world more clearly? • How do writers comment on adult experiences through the more innocent eyes of a child? • How has the 'coming-of-age' genre developed over time?

Texts

Throughout Quest, students will encounter a wide variety of texts from different authors, genres, forms (written and spoken) and time periods that:

- will develop and empower them as readers, writers and communicators
- are from writers who reflect, challenge and broaden students' identities and experiences
- cover a broad variety of topics and themes
- are diverse and representative
- unlock new worlds and offer insights into their own experiences
- build their background knowledge and self-discovery
- are high-quality and appropriate for study.

Quest pathways

Core curriculum pathway	Alternative curriculum pathway	Assessment	Planning and delivery	CPD
Student Book	Kerboodle	Kerboodle	Teacher Book and Kerboodle	Kerboodle
Chapter 1: Power and influence Units 1–4 Chapter 1: Power and influence Units 5–8	Alternative source texts and activities for each unit, delivering the same learning outcomes	Mini-checkpoint quizzes at the end of each unit to review students' knowledge. Checkpoint assessments to assess students' application of their knowledge, using their reading, writing or speaking and listening skills after Units 4 and 8. Spelling, grammar and punctuation quizzes to be used as a diagnostic tool or as a learning review tool after a specific grammar lesson.	Long-term plans Medium-term chapter plans Short-term unit plans Lesson delivery support: teacher notes and slides	Course and subject delivery support English subject knowledge and pedagogy
Chapter 2: Terror and wonder Units 1–4 Chapter 2: Terror and wonder Units 5–8	Alternative source texts and activities for each unit, delivering the same learning outcomes	Mini-checkpoint quizzes at the end of each unit to review students' knowledge. Checkpoint assessments to assess students' application of their knowledge, using their reading, writing or speaking and listening skills after Units 4 and 8. Spelling, grammar and punctuation quizzes to be used as a diagnostic tool or as a learning review tool after a specific grammar lesson.		
Chapter 3: Wild places and urban landscapes Units 1–4 Chapter 3: Wild places and urban landscapes Units 5–8	Alternative source texts and activities for each unit, delivering the same learning outcomes	Mini-checkpoint quizzes at the end of each unit to review students' knowledge. Checkpoint assessments to assess students' application of their knowledge, using their reading, writing or speaking and listening skills after Units 4 and 8. Spelling, grammar and punctuation quizzes to be used as a diagnostic tool or as a learning review tool after a specific grammar lesson.		

The core pathway

The core pathway is delivered through the Student Book. The Student Book has three chapters, each covering one big theme.

Each chapter has eight units of work, grouped into two parts. Each part has a different focus, e.g. Units 1–4 might cover fiction and Units 5–8 might be on non-fiction. Each individual unit also has a particular skills focus: reading, writing or speaking and listening.

A unit will take approximately two or three lessons, depending on how it is taught. This makes the course flexible enough to fit into a school's timetable and to allow for a more personalised approach to teaching and learning.

Alternative pathway

There are additional source texts and activities on Kerboodle, offering a choice of resources that can be selected as appropriate for particular students.

Using the Quest Student Book

Student Books 1, 2 and 3 correspond to the three years at KS3. The first unit in Student Book 1 builds on the knowledge students have from KS2 and introduces a variety of texts that they experience in their lives and then looks at specific text types and themes. Books 2 and 3 develop students' knowledge and skills further and prepare them for English at KS4.

Each chapter in the Student Book starts with a chapter opener that activates prior knowledge and informs students about what they will be learning.

The learning overview supports metacognition by preparing students for what they will be learning and will help them to monitor what they have learned. It also shows a coherent learning pathway through the Student Book.

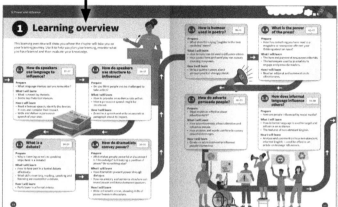

Big idea: gives an overview of what the unit is about and why it is important. It can also include links to previous units as a reminder of what students already know.

Key terms: are flagged the first time they appear in a chapter and include technical or literary terms.

Learning objectives: focus on what students will be learning and how they will demonstrate their understanding. The first objective is about what students will learn, the second is about what they are exploring, investigating or considering further, and the third objective is to write, analyse or present what they have learned.

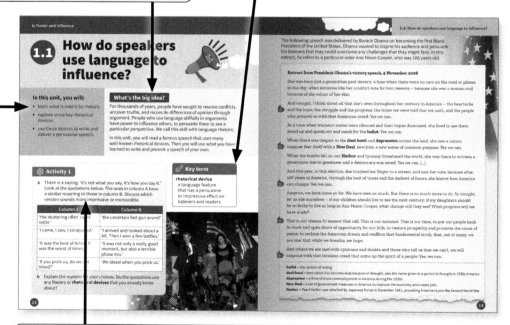

Metacognitive activities: require students to think about what they already know about the text, the theme or the skills they'll be using.

Boosting your vocabulary: activities and strategies to help students work out unfamiliar words, along with opportunities for them to practise using the words in their own writing.

Building your knowledge: introduces the knowledge focus of the unit in the context of the source text. Students are encouraged to think about what they already know and understand about the focus of the unit, drawing on their own experiences.

Tips: remind students of a connection to another key piece of knowledge or key skill, and give prompts.

Writing icon: shows when students are expected to write their answer or response to the activity. All other parts of the activity can be used to prompt a discussion or a whole-class written response.

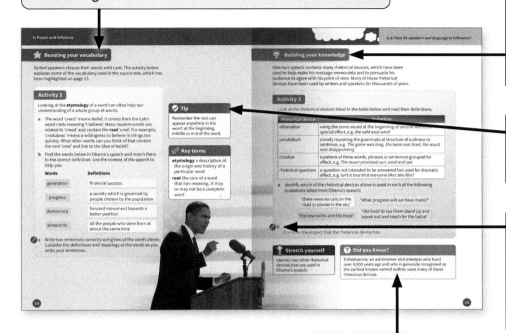

Did you know?: offers short and snappy facts to aid or add to students' comprehension of a text.

Putting it all together: all of the tasks in the unit build towards students completing an activity that will allow them to demonstrate they have understood the skills and knowledge covered.

Modelled answers: can be used to support students with their own writing or responses.

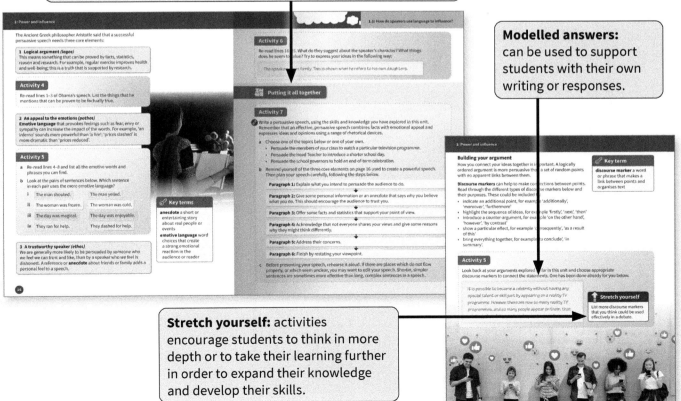

Stretch yourself: activities encourage students to think in more depth or to take their learning further in order to expand their knowledge and develop their skills.

Using the Quest Teacher Book

The Teacher Book supports the planning and implementation of Quest, using the Quest Student Book and Kerboodle resources. For every chapter of Quest, the Teacher Book contains:

- an introduction to the topic
- guidance on how to use the chapter openers
- unit-by-unit overviews with flexible lesson activities.

> The chapter overview grid outlines the eight units: the skills focus, source texts, alternative source texts on Kerboodle and objectives.

> The chapter introduction includes icons linked to the *Oxford Smart* curriculum pillars, showing how the pillars have been embedded into Quest.

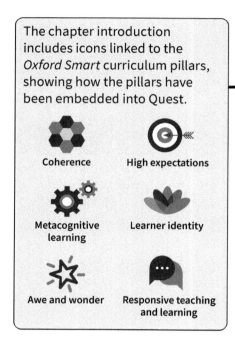

Coherence

High expectations

Metacognitive learning

Learner identity

Awe and wonder

Responsive teaching and learning

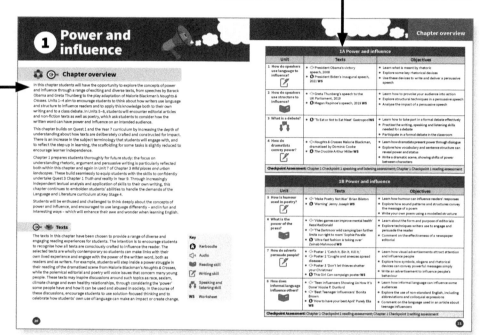

> These pages help to explain the chapter and the topic in more detail, giving guidance on making cross-curricular links and building students' background knowledge.

> Mini-checkpoints can be assigned after every unit to review students' knowledge. There are checkpoint assessments at the end of each part of the chapter, after Units 4 and 8. Spelling, grammar and punctuation quizzes can also be used to support lessons or individual students as needed. Please refer to pages 16–17 for more information on assessment in Quest.

> Suggestions for further reading, either for class novels and playscripts, or for students to read on their own, are included in every chapter.

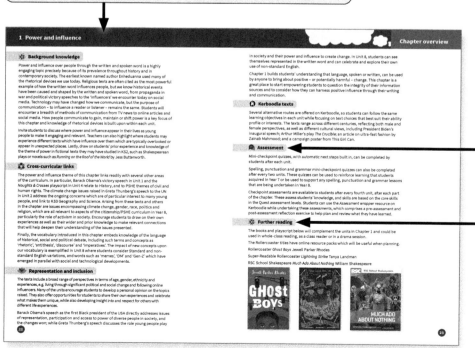

This is guidance on how to use the Student Book chapter openers and learning overviews. These openers help to engage students with the topic of the chapter, to show them what they will be learning and to activate prior learning. The information on these pages will help to guide students in completing the metacognitive activities that will support their understanding of the learning in the Student Book.

Key vocabulary links to the theme and will help to support students in accessing the texts.

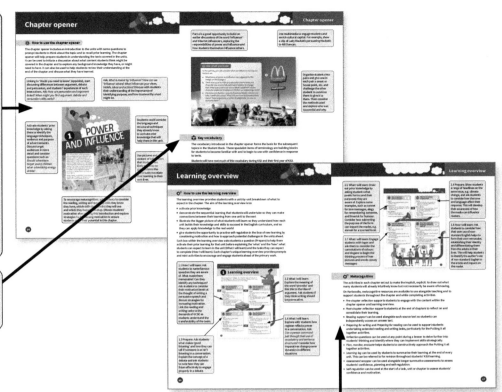

The unit focus offers an overview of objectives, texts and key terms covered in that unit. Before starting, it may help to spend time explaining the key terms to make sure that students are familiar with them before they encounter them in the unit.

Metacognition highlights how Kerboodle metacognition templates and resources can be used to support students' learning and help them to constructively approach activities.

This box indicates where the alternative text provided on Kerboodle could be used rather than the source text in the Student Book.

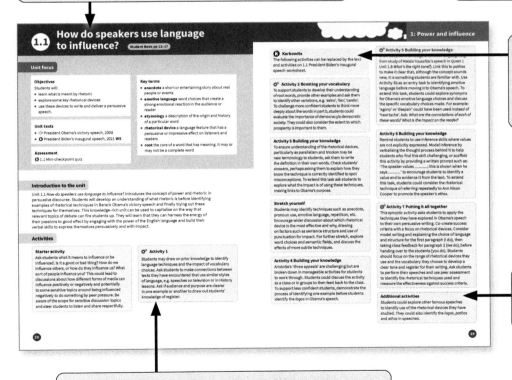

There are additional activities that can be used to support, extend or for homework.

The activities follow the sequence of the Student Book and support the learning with guidance on implementation, metacognitive strategies, support and extension ideas and possible homework activities.

Kerboodle

Oxford Smart Quest Kerboodle provides additional teaching and learning resources, as well as a comprehensive assessment package. Resources include worksheets with alternative texts, audio, automatically marked assessments, books, and the CPD and Research Hub.

Kerboodle is online, allowing teachers and students to access the course anytime and anywhere. Homework and assessments can be set through the Assessment system and progress can be tracked using the Markbook.

Kerboodle book

The *Oxford Smart* Quest Kerboodle book provides a digital copy of the Student Book for use at the front of the classroom or for students to access independently.

Teacher access to the Kerboodle book is automatically available as part of the Resources and Assessment package.

A set of tools is available with the Kerboodle book, allowing teachers to personalise their book and make notes.

Like all other resources offered on Kerboodle, the Kerboodle book can be accessed on a range of devices.

Use different tools such as sticky notes, bookmarks and pen features to personalise each page.

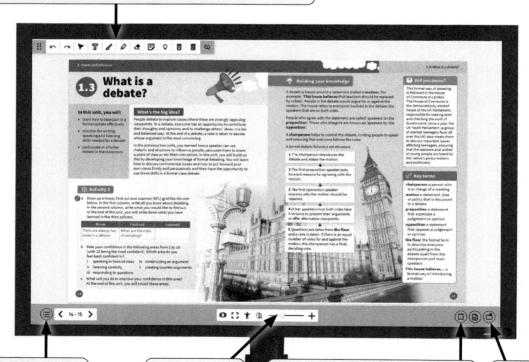

Navigate around the book quickly with the contents menu, key word search or page number search.

Zoom in and spotlight text.

Every teacher and student has their own digital notebook for use within their Kerboodle book. You can choose to share your notes with students or hide them from view – all student notes are accessible to themselves only.

All the associated resources can be viewed on each spread.

Resources

Click the Resources tab to access the full list of *Oxford Smart* Quest lesson resources. The resources section includes:

- documents containing the texts from the Student Book
- audio recordings of all the text extracts from the Student Book
- lesson notes for use when teaching – these are a version of what's in the Teacher Book

- PowerPoint slides to help with lesson delivery
- worksheets containing additional texts to replace or supplement the source texts in the Student Book
- metacognition resources and templates to use with students throughout the Student Book and while undertaking activities.

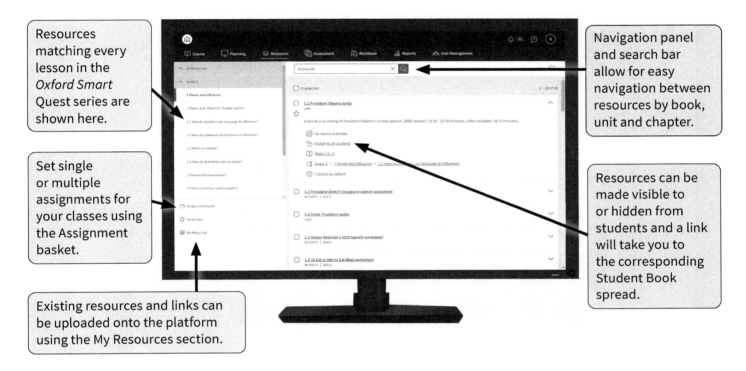

Resources matching every lesson in the *Oxford Smart* Quest series are shown here.

Set single or multiple assignments for your classes using the Assignment basket.

Existing resources and links can be uploaded onto the platform using the My Resources section.

Navigation panel and search bar allow for easy navigation between resources by book, unit and chapter.

Resources can be made visible to or hidden from students and a link will take you to the corresponding Student Book spread.

Worksheets and alternative texts

These alternative texts provide a flexible approach to teaching the objectives for the unit, allowing the teacher to tailor the curriculum to different needs: more accessible and relevant texts, challenging texts and more diversity.

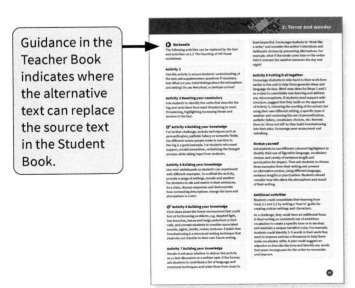

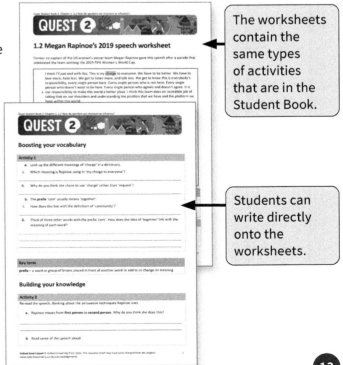

Guidance in the Teacher Book indicates where the alternative text can replace the source text in the Student Book.

The worksheets contain the same types of activities that are in the Student Book.

Students can write directly onto the worksheets.

Kerboodle

Assessment and Markbook

All the assessment material on Kerboodle has been developed alongside the curriculum and resources. Clicking on the Assessment tab will reveal a range of materials to help deliver a varied, motivating and effective assessment programme.

It is easy to import class registers and create user accounts for students. Once the class is set up, assessments can be assigned for students to do individually or as a group. They can also complete them at home.

The Markbook with a reporting function helps to keep track of students' results. This includes both automarked assessment and work that needs to be teacher-marked.

You can find out more about the Assessment framework on page 17.

In the Assessment tab, you can find mini-checkpoints for each lesson, checkpoints for each chapter and end-of-unit assessments for each unit.

The Markbook and reporting function helps you track your students' progress.

Reports can be generated using data from the checkpoints and mini-checkpoints.

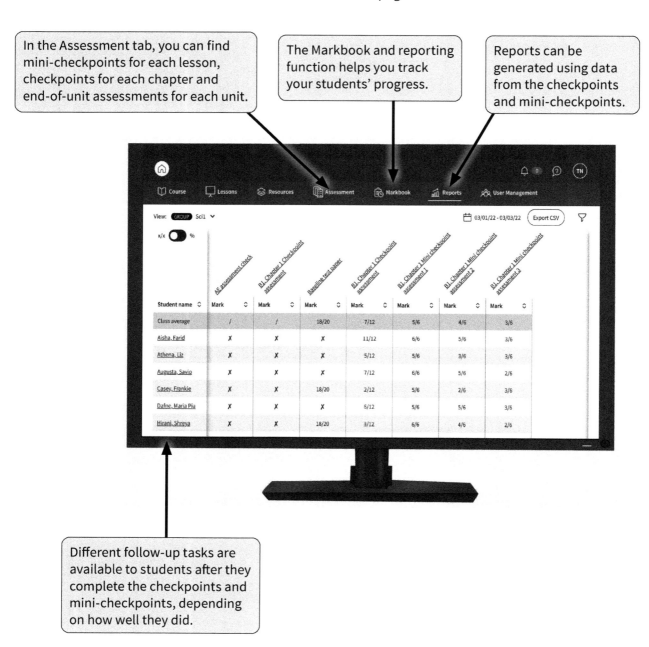

Different follow-up tasks are available to students after they complete the checkpoints and mini-checkpoints, depending on how well they did.

Kerboodle Research Library

The Research Library contains:

- the pedagogical research and evidence that have been drawn on when developing the Quest resources, as well as more information on the *Oxford Smart* Curriculum and the six pillars that underpin it
- summaries of other wider pedagogical research that impacts the current and future classroom, such as vocabulary and word gap reports, the various aspects of reading, oracy, grammar and metacognition.

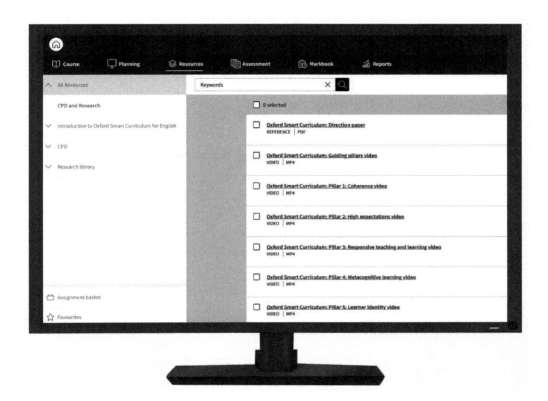

Continuing professional development

Alongside the Research Library, CPD resources will support implementation of Quest.

These resources include blogs, articles and videos and will be delivered in easy-to-access modules that can be undertaken by individuals or groups, depending on how each school plans and delivers their CPD sessions. The resources will cover the pillars of the *Oxford Smart* Curriculum, how to use the Quest resources in the classroom, and other relevant topics, such as vocabulary and oracy.

Impact

The extensive testing of Quest within pioneer schools has informed the content of the course. This link to schools and future research will help continually update and review Quest to provide an up-to-date and relevant course.

The Research Library will also continue to be updated as the body of research grows to support the implementation of effective pedagogy in the classroom.

Assessment

Quest's assessment model combines regular formative and summative assessments along with low-stakes quizzing that aims to interrupt the forgetting curve and ensures that students have grasped key concepts.

Student Book 2 example assessment journey

	Chapter								End of year
	Unit 1	Unit 2	Unit 3	Unit 4	Unit 5	Unit 6	Unit 7	Unit 8	
Mini-checkpoints	✓	✓	✓	✓	✓	✓	✓	✓	
Checkpoints				✓				✓	
Reactivate quizzes	Triggered by mini-checkpoints								
End of year assessment									✓

Mini-checkpoints

These automarked quizzes at the end of each unit of the Student Book will test that students have acquired and understood the knowledge introduced in that unit.

Following each mini-checkpoint, students will be presented with a personalised next step that will either support them to achieve 'secure', or provide challenge questions to reach 'extending'.

Additional grammar, punctuation and spelling quizzes throughout Quest target areas that need more explicit teaching, misconceptions or gaps in learning.

Reactivate quizzes

These automarked retrieval quizzes will be automatically triggered each time a student completes a mini-checkpoint quiz, and will recap the knowledge that students have covered.

Checkpoints

Units of work in the Student Book will build to half-termly checkpoint assessments that allow students to put their skills into practice. These checkpoints will follow the assessment framework developed for *Oxford Smart* Curriculum for English (available on Kerboodle), allowing teachers to assess, record and track the progress of all students across the nine chapters of Student Books 1–3 in the core skills of reading, writing, and speaking and listening.

The *Assessment wrapper* resource on Kerboodle helps students when undertaking the checkpoint assessments at the end of Units 4 and 8 in each chapter. It comprises a pre-assessment reflection that encourages students to think about self-regulation of learning, comprehension and planning of the assessments, and success criteria, as well as a post-assessment reflection that encourages students to review their work, identifying their strengths and weaknesses, and ask for further support in future tasks.

Tracking progress

The mini-checkpoint quizzes and half-termly checkpoint assessments will help to identify and assess where students are developing, secure and extending their knowledge and skills.

- Developing: learners are working towards secure knowledge and understanding but need more support to achieve this.
- Secure: learners have a secure knowledge and understanding; this is the aspiration for all learners to achieve, prior to moving on to the next topic.
- Extending: learners are working beyond age-related expectation, and their knowledge and understanding can be stretched and challenged.

Assessment descriptors

<table>
<tr><td rowspan="4">Reading</td><td>Retrieval (R1)</td><td>Retrieve and summarise information and ideas from texts; select appropriate references and use these references to support a point of view.</td></tr>
<tr><td>Interpretation (R2)</td><td>Understand ideas and perspectives in texts; make inferences and interpretations; identify and interpret the context of texts. Evaluate the significance of texts.</td></tr>
<tr><td>Methods (R3)</td><td>Understand that texts are deliberate constructs; explore the effects of the methods writers use to create texts; comment on and evaluate the impact of methods on the text as a whole, using a range of subject terms appropriately.</td></tr>
<tr><td>Comparison (R4)</td><td>Make links between information and ideas from different texts; comment on and evaluate the relationships between texts. Compare writers' perspectives in different texts, including how writers use different methods for different purposes and audiences.</td></tr>
<tr><td rowspan="4">Writing</td><td>Communicating ideas (W1)</td><td>Generate, select and develop ideas; communicate ideas and perspectives effectively using different forms and genres. Write engagingly for different purposes and audiences.</td></tr>
<tr><td>Structure and organisation (W2)</td><td>Plan, draft and organise writing effectively, using cohesive sentences and paragraphs, sequencing and developing ideas coherently and using a range of structural features.</td></tr>
<tr><td>Crafting (W3)</td><td>Create texts using varied tone, style and register and using vocabulary accurately and appropriately. Craft writing using a range of linguistic methods to produce increasingly complex texts using a range of rhetorical and narrative methods.</td></tr>
<tr><td>Accuracy (W4)</td><td>Use sentence forms to create impact and punctuation to convey meaning. Spell increasingly complex words accurately and use grammatical constructions in a controlled way.</td></tr>
<tr><td rowspan="4">Speaking and listening</td><td>Voice (S1)</td><td>Speak audibly and confidently in a range of situations, varying the pace and tone of speaking. Project voice to engage an audience and use body language and facial expression appropriately.</td></tr>
<tr><td>Vocabulary (S2)</td><td>Use an appropriate range of vocabulary and grammatical constructions when talking, adopting an appropriate register and/or style for audience and purpose. Use rhetorical/linguistic techniques appropriate to the task.</td></tr>
<tr><td>Organisation (S3)</td><td>Plan and structure talk effectively for a range of audiences and purposes, using a range of methods, maintaining focus and managing time. Monitor and continually evaluate the impact of talk.</td></tr>
<tr><td>Collaboration (S4)</td><td>Take turns when talking and manage interactions, listening actively and responding appropriately. Use questions to seek information and clarification and give reasons to support own views and to build on or challenge others' contributions.</td></tr>
</table>

End-of-year assessment

At the end of each year there will be a summative assessment, available either as a digital or paper-based assessment.

Metacognition

What is metacognition?

To help students become increasingly independent and confident learners, teachers need to facilitate students' understanding of their own strengths and weaknesses and the strategies that they use to learn. Metacognition is about teaching students to be strategic learners. A metacognitive learner may consider their motivation towards learning and how this impacts their effort and progress; they may consciously plan how to approach a task, monitor how it's going, and evaluate how they can improve on their learning in the future. Metacognitive learners are supported by teachers to set their own meaningful goals, identify and utilise the strategies that work for them, and self-reflect on their effectiveness. Teachers can enable learners to become more metacognitive through: their approach to planning and delivering lessons; developing a growth mindset in students; making explicit the learning processes they themselves go through as 'experts', so that students can see how to progress. There are many strategies teachers can employ to improve the metacognition of learners in their classroom and this guide aims to:

- introduce the Plan, Monitor, Evaluate (PME) cycle
- support teachers with understanding the seven stages of developing metacognition explicitly as developed by the Education Endowment Foundation (EEF).

The Plan, Monitor, Evaluate (PME) cycle

The Plan, Monitor, Evaluate (PME) cycle is a core part of metacognition and helps students regulate their learning by building their knowledge of themselves as learners and of specific strategies or tasks. This cycle forms a structured reflection process that students can follow when completing a task or undertaking independent study.

1 **Planning (before the task):** During this phase of the cycle, students think about the goal of the task ahead, reflecting on the subject knowledge required, and whether specific strategies need to be used. They should consider things like whether they have done a similar task before and whether they have experience that they can use to be successful now.

2 **Monitoring (during the task):** During this phase, students review their progress against the goals of the task. This could mean that they reflect on whether their chosen strategy is successful and make any necessary changes.

3 **Evaluation (end of the task):** During this phase, students evaluate the effectiveness of their plan. They can review the strengths and weaknesses of what they produced and reflect on whether they would do anything differently next time.

Teaching the PME cycle

One way to approach teaching this is to use a regulatory checklist. This is a series of questions that guide students through each phase. These questions can be introduced to students so that they understand why the PME cycle is effective and how they can use it. In practice, it may be more appropriate to focus on one of the phases first, rather than the whole checklist, or to have the whole class reflect on the questions as a group, rather than individually. Over time, through guided practice, students will become more independent, leading to the PME cycle naturally becoming the way that they approach new tasks.

Planning

- What are your starting points for learning?
- What do you already know about the theme/genre/skill/feature?
- How confident do you feel about an activity or text?
- Do you need to recap anything?
- What similar tasks have been completed previously? What strategies worked well and what could be improved?
- Have you got or are you going to plan any success criteria?

Monitoring

- What could you do to check your work and improve it?
- How confident are you with the task?
- Is the strategy you are using working?
- How do you know that the strategy is working?
- Is your answer meeting the success criteria?

Evaluation

- What went well?
- What strategies worked successfully?
- What might you change for next time?
- What do you still need to know?
- What knowledge would have made this better?
- What could you do to meet any particular success criteria?

The EEF seven-step guide

The Education Endowment Foundation suggests following the seven-step approach to teaching metacognitive skills. This seven-step approach can be used as a planning tool to support the delivery of any new skill or strategy, and can be used in all aspects of learning.

1 Activate prior knowledge
2 Explicit strategy instruction
3 Modelling of learned strategy
4 Memorisation of strategy
5 Guided practice
6 Independent practice
7 Structured reflection

Metacognition in Quest

Metacognitive activities are indicated in both the Student Book and Teacher Book with an icon, so it is easy to see when metacognition is being covered.

 The icon in the Teacher Book reflects the links of the *Oxford Smart* Curriculum to pillar 4: support engaged, self-regulated and metacognitive learning. It indicates that, in that part of the Student Book, students are learning or being encouraged to use metacognitive strategies.

 The icon in the Student Book indicates where an activity is using a metacognitive strategy.

Metacognition resources on Kerboodle

On Kerboodle, the following metacognitive resources are available to use alongside teaching and to support students throughout their learning of each chapter:

- Pre-chapter reflection
- Post-chapter reflection
- Reading support
- Preparing for writing and Preparing for reading
- Reflection questions
- Plan, monitor, evaluate
- Learning log
- Assessment wrapper
- Self-regulation

1 Power and influence

Chapter overview

In this chapter students will have the opportunity to explore the concepts of power and influence through a range of exciting and diverse texts, from speeches by Barack Obama and Greta Thunberg to the play adaptation of Malorie Blackman's *Noughts & Crosses*. Units 1–4 aim to encourage students to think about how writers use language and structure to influence readers and to apply this knowledge both to their own writing and to a class debate. In Units 5–8, students will encounter editorial articles and non-fiction texts as well as poetry, which ask students to consider how the written word can have power and influence on an intended audience.

This chapter builds on Quest 1 and the Year 7 curriculum by increasing the depth of understanding about how texts are deliberately crafted and constructed for impact. There is an increase in the subject terminology that students will engage with, and to reflect the step up in learning, the scaffolding for some tasks is slightly reduced to encourage learner independence.

Chapter 1 prepares students thoroughly for future study: the focus on understanding rhetoric, argument and persuasive writing is particularly reflected both within this chapter and again in Unit 7 of Chapter 3 *Wild places and urban landscapes*. These build seamlessly to equip students with the skills to confidently undertake Quest 3 Chapter 1 *Truth and reality* in Year 9. Through increasingly independent textual analysis and application of skills to their own writing, this chapter continues to embolden students' abilities to handle the demands of the Language and Literature curriculum at Key Stage 4.

Students will be enthused and challenged to think deeply about the concepts of power and influence, and encouraged to use language differently – and in fun and interesting ways – which will enhance their awe and wonder when learning English.

Texts

The texts in this chapter have been chosen to provide a range of diverse and engaging reading experiences for students. The intention is to encourage students to recognise how all texts are consciously crafted to influence the reader. The selected texts are wholly contemporary so students can make links with their own lived experience and engage with the power of the written word, both as readers and as writers. For example, students will step inside a power struggle in their reading of the dramatised scene from Malorie Blackman's *Noughts & Crosses*, while the polemical editorial and poetry will voice issues that concern many young people. These texts may inspire discussions around such topics as race, sexism, climate change and even healthy relationships, through considering the 'power' some people have and how it can be used and abused in society. In the course of these discussions, encourage students to use solution-focused thinking and to celebrate how students' own use of language can make an impact or create change.

Key

 k Kerboodle

 Audio

 Reading skill

 Writing skill

 Speaking and listening skill

WS Worksheet

1A Power and influence

Unit	Texts	Objectives
1 How do speakers use language to influence?	• 🔊 President Obama's victory speech, 2008 • Ⓚ President Biden's inaugural speech, 2021 **WS**	• Learn what is meant by rhetoric • Explore some key rhetorical devices • Use these devices to write and deliver a persuasive speech
2 How do speakers use structure to influence?	• 🔊 Greta Thunberg's speech to the UK Parliament, 2019 • Ⓚ Megan Rapinoe's speech, 2019 **WS**	• Learn how to provoke your audience into action • Explore structural techniques in a persuasive speech • Analyse the impact of a persuasive speech
3 What is a debate?	• Ⓚ 'To Eat or Not to Eat Meat' Gastropod **WS**	• Learn how to take part in a formal debate effectively • Practise the writing, speaking and listening skills needed for a debate • Participate in a formal debate in the classroom
4 How do dramatists convey power?	• 🔊 *Noughts & Crosses* Malorie Blackman, dramatised by Dominic Cooke • Ⓚ *The Crucible* Arthur Miller **WS**	• Learn how dramatists present power through dialogue • Explore how vocabulary and sentence structure can reveal power and status • Write a dramatic scene, showing shifts of power between characters

Checkpoint Assessment: Chapter 1 Checkpoint 1 speaking and listening assessment; Chapter 1 Checkpoint 1 reading assessment

1B Power and influence

Unit	Texts	Objectives
5 How is humour used in poetry?	• 🔊 'Make Poetry Not War' Brian Bilston • Ⓚ 'Warning' Jenny Joseph **WS**	• Learn how humour can influence readers' responses • Explore how sound patterns and structures convey the message of a poem • Write your own poem using a modelled structure
6 What is the power of the press?	• 🔊 'Video games can improve mental health' Keza MacDonald • 🔊 'The Dartmoor wild camping ban further limits our right to roam' Sophie Pavelle • Ⓚ 'Ultra-fast fashion is taking over' Zainab Mahmood **WS**	• Learn about the form and purpose of editorials • Explore techniques writers use to engage and persuade the reader • Comment on the effectiveness of a newspaper editorial
7 How do adverts persuade people?	• 🔊 Poster 1 'Catch it. Bin it. Kill it.' • 🔊 Poster 2 'Coughs and sneezes spread diseases' • 🔊 Poster 3 'Don't let thieves shatter your Christmas' • Ⓚ This Girl Can campaign poster **WS**	• Learn how visual advertisements attract attention and influence people • Explore how symbols, slogans and rhetorical devices can convey powerful messages simply • Write an advertisement to influence people's behaviour
8 How does informal language influence others?	• 🔊 'Teen Influencers Showing Us How It's Done' Nicole P. Dunford • 🔊 'Best Teenager Influencers' Bonita Brown • Ⓚ 'How to have your best April' Purely Ella **WS**	• Learn how informal language can influence some audiences • Explore the use of non-standard English, including abbreviations and colloquial expressions • Comment on the language used in an article about teenage influencers

Checkpoint Assessment: Chapter 1 Checkpoint 2 reading assessment; Chapter 1 Checkpoint 2 writing assessment

✲ Background knowledge

Power and influence over people through the written and spoken word is a highly engaging topic precisely because of its prevalence throughout history and in contemporary society. The earliest known named author Enheduanna used many of the rhetorical devices we use today. Religious texts are often cited as the most powerful example of how the written word influences people, but we know historical events have been caused and shaped by the written and spoken word, from propaganda in war and political victory speeches to the 'influencers' we encounter today on social media. Technology may have changed how we communicate, but the purpose of communication – to influence a reader or listener – remains the same. Students will encounter a breadth of methods of communication from TV news to online articles and social media. How people communicate to gain, maintain or shift power is a key focus of this chapter and knowledge of rhetorical devices is built upon within each unit.

Invite students to discuss where power and influence appear in their lives as young people to make it engaging and relevant. Teachers can also highlight where students may experience different texts which have influence over them which are typically overlooked or appear in unexpected places. Lastly, draw on students' prior experience and knowledge of the theme of power in fictional texts they may have studied in KS2, such as Shakespearean plays or novels such as *Running on the Roof of the World* by Jess Butterworth.

◈ Cross-curricular links

The power and influence theme of this chapter links readily with several other areas of the curriculum. In particular, Barack Obama's victory speech in Unit 1 and the *Noughts & Crosses* playscript in Unit 4 relate to History, and to PSHE themes of civil and human rights. The climate change issues raised in Greta Thunberg's speech to the UN in Unit 2 address the ongoing concerns which are of particular interest to many young people, and link to KS3 Geography and Science. Arising from these texts and others in the chapter are issues encompassing climate change, gender, race, politics and religion, which are all relevant to aspects of the citizenship/PSHE curriculum in Year 8, particularly the role of activism in society. Encourage students to draw on their own experiences as well as their wider and prior knowledge to make relevant connections that will help deepen their understanding of the issues presented.

Finally, the vocabulary introduced in this chapter embeds knowledge of the language of historical, social and political debate, including such terms and concepts as 'rhetoric', 'antithesis', 'discourse' and 'imperatives'. The impact of new concepts upon our vocabulary is exemplified in Unit 8 where students consider Standard and non-standard English variations, and words such as 'memes', 'DM' and 'Gen-Z' which have emerged in parallel with social and technological developments.

Representation and inclusion

The texts include a broad range of perspectives in terms of age, gender, ethnicity and experiences, e.g. living through significant political and social change and following online influencers. Many of the units encourage students to develop a personal opinion on the topics raised. They also offer opportunities for students to share their own experiences and celebrate what makes them unique, while also developing insight into and respect for others with different life experiences.

Barack Obama's speech as the first Black president of the USA directly addresses issues of representation, participation and access to power of diverse people in society, and the changes won; while Greta Thunberg's speech discusses the role young people play in society and their power and influence to create change. In Unit 8, students can see themselves represented in the written word and can celebrate and explore their own use of non-standard English.

Chapter 1 builds students' understanding that language, spoken or written, can be used by anyone to bring about positive – or potentially harmful – change. This chapter is a great place to start empowering students to question the integrity of their information sources and to consider how they can harness positive influence through their writing and communication.

Kerboodle texts

Several alternative routes are offered on Kerboodle, so students can follow the same learning objectives in each unit while focusing on text choices that best suit their ability profile or interests. The texts range across different centuries, reflecting both male and female perspectives, as well as different cultural views, including President Biden's inaugural speech; Arthur Miller's play *The Crucible;* an article on ultra-fast fashion by Zainab Mahmood; and a campaign poster from This Girl Can.

Assessment

Mini-checkpoint quizzes, with automatic next steps built in, can be completed by students after each unit.

Spelling, punctuation and grammar mini-checkpoint quizzes can also be completed after every two units. These quizzes can be used to reinforce learning that students acquired in Year 7 or be used to support any spelling, punctuation and grammar lessons that are being undertaken in Year 8.

Checkpoint assessments are available to students after every fourth unit, after each part of the chapter. These assess students' knowledge, and skills are based on the core skills in the Quest assessment levels. Students can use the *Assessment wrapper* resource on Kerboodle while undertaking these assessments, which comprises a pre-assessment and post-assessment reflection exercise to help plan and review what they have learned.

Further reading

The books and playscript below will complement the units in Chapter 1 and could be used in whole-class reading, as a class reader or in a drama session.

The Rollercoaster titles have online resource packs which will be useful when planning.

Rollercoaster *Ghost Boys* Jewell Parker Rhodes

Super-Readable Rollercoaster *Lightning Strike* Tanya Landman

RSC School Shakespeare *Much Ado About Nothing* William Shakespeare

Chapter opener

The chapter opener includes an introduction to the units with some questions to prompt students to think about the topic and to recall prior learning. The chapter opener will help prepare students in understanding the texts covered in the units. It can be used to initiate a discussion about what content students think might be covered in the chapter and to explore any background knowledge they have, or might need to have. It can also be used to help students review their understanding at the end of the chapter and discuss what they have learned.

> Linking to 'Words you need to know' (opposite), start discussing differences between argument, debate and persuasion, and students' experiences of such interactions. Ask: *How are persuasion and argument linked? When might you find argument, debate and persuasion skills useful?*

> Ask: *What is meant by 'influence'? How can we 'influence' others? What influences your views, beliefs, ideas and actions?* Discuss with students their understanding of the importance of identifying purpose, and how trustworthy a text might be.

> Activate students' prior knowledge by asking them to identify the language techniques, audience and purpose of advertisements. Discuss target audiences in more detail and consider questions such as: *Should advertisers target young children when advertising energy drinks?*

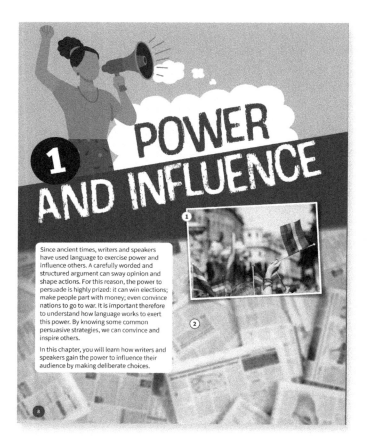

> Students could consider the language and structural techniques they already know to activate prior knowledge that will help them in this unit.

> Use pictures and content of influencers that students are likely to follow to give students the opportunity to relate their learning to their own lives.

> To encourage metacognition, ask students to consider the reading, writing and speaking skills they know they have, which skills they predict they will use and which they hope to develop. Discuss students' motivation after reading this introduction and explore strategies for harnessing motivation to ensure students meet their potential in this chapter.

Part a is a good opportunity to build on earlier discussions of the word 'influence' and Internet influencers, exploring the responsibilities of power and influence and how students themselves influence others.

Use multimedia to engage students and enrich cultural capital. For example, show a clip of Lady Macbeth persuading Macbeth to kill Duncan.

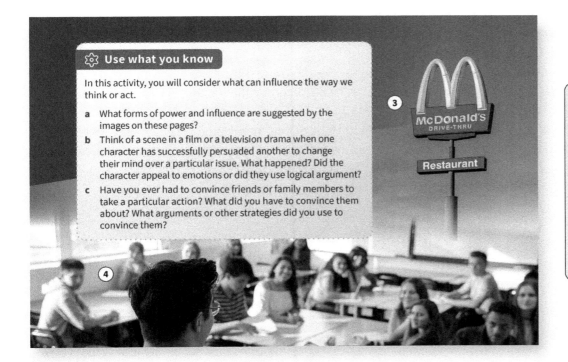

⚙ Use what you know

In this activity, you will consider what can influence the way we think or act.

a What forms of power and influence are suggested by the images on these pages?

b Think of a scene in a film or a television drama when one character has successfully persuaded another to change their mind over a particular issue. What happened? Did the character appeal to emotions or did they use logical argument?

c Have you ever had to convince friends or family members to take a particular action? What did you have to convince them about? What arguments or other strategies did you use to convince them?

Organise students into pairs and give one in each pair a sweet or house point, etc. and challenge the other student to convince them to give it to them. Then consider the methods used and explore who was successful and why.

✿ Key vocabulary

The vocabulary introduced in the chapter opener forms the basis for the subsequent topics in the Student Book. These specialist items of terminology are building blocks for students to become familiar with and to begin to use with confidence in response to texts.

Students will have met much of this vocabulary during KS2 and their first year of KS3. However, some students may struggle to visualise the more abstract concepts. Visual reminders on classroom wall displays may help, as well as providing definitions to reinforce the meanings.

Explore the chapter's key words through activities:

1 Use Frayer diagrams to explore these words.
2 Find images to go with each word.
3 Use each word in a sentence.
4 Explore morphology of some words. For example, what does the suffix 'ist' indicate?
5 Which can be nouns, which are adjectives, which are verbs? How does changing the word class ('persuasion' to 'persuasive', for example) alter the connotations?
6 Do any of the careers associated with these words appeal to students? Why?

Words you need to know

argument, debate, persuasion, rhetoric, dramatist, journalist, activist, influencer

Learning overview

The learning overview provides students with a unit-by-unit breakdown of what to expect in the chapter. The aim of the learning overview is to:

- activate prior knowledge
- demonstrate the sequential learning that students will undertake so they can make connections between their learning from one unit to the next
- illustrate the bigger picture of what students will learn so they understand how each unit builds their knowledge and skills to succeed in the English curriculum, and so they can apply knowledge to the real world
- give students the opportunity to practise self-regulation in the face of new learning by considering motivation and how to approach potential challenges in the units ahead.

Each box within the learning overview asks students a question (Prepare) to help them activate their prior learning for that unit before explaining the 'what' and the 'how': what students can expect to learn in the unit (What I will learn) and the tasks they can expect to complete (How I will learn). Each chapter's unique learning overview provides prompts and mini-activities to encourage and engage students ahead of the primary work.

1.1 How I will learn: Ask students to name famous speeches they are aware of. What made them memorable? Can they identify any techniques? Ask students to consider their motivation levels at the thought of writing a persuasive speech and discuss strategies for increasing motivation. Link the reading and writing tasks to the demands of GCSE so students understand the transferability of the tasks.

1.2 What I will learn: Explore the meaning of the word 'provoke' and link this to the idea of argument. Ask students if they think writing should be provocative.

1.3 Prepare: Ask students what makes 'good listening' and how they can tell if someone is or isn't listening in a conversation. Explain the concept of a debate and ask students to note how they can listen effectively to engage properly in a debate.

1.4 What I will learn: Explore with students how register reflects power in a conversation. Ask: *Can a person command just through their use of vocabulary and sentence structures?* Consider how imperatives change power dynamics in different situations.

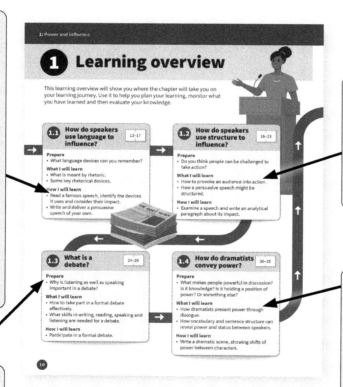

1.5 What I will learn: Draw out prior knowledge by asking students what poetic forms (and their purposes) they are aware of. Explore some examples, such as sonnet for love messages, elegy for remembering someone, and limerick for humour. Consider how subverting the purpose of the form can impact the reader, e.g. sonnet for a scorned lover.

1.7 What I will learn: Engage students with logos and ask them to consider the connotations of colours and slogans to begin the thinking process of how pictures and words convey messages.

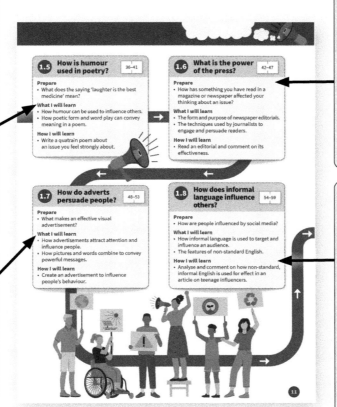

1.6 Prepare: Show students a range of headlines on the same issue, e.g. climate change, and ask students to consider how the tone and language affect their response. This will develop their awareness of how the media can influence readers.

1.8 How I will learn: Ask students to consider how their own use of non-standard English helps to form their own vernacular, establishing their identity and differentiating them from the adults in their lives. This will help students to identify the author's use of non-standard English in the article and impact on the reader.

⚙️ Metacognition

The activities in each chapter set out to make the implicit, explicit: to draw out what many students will already intuitively know but not necessarily be aware of knowing.

On Kerboodle, metacognitive resources are available to use alongside teaching and to support students throughout the chapter and while completing activities.

- *Pre-chapter reflection* supports students to engage with the content within the chapter opener and learning overview.
- *Post-chapter reflection* supports students at the end of chapters to reflect on and consolidate their learning.
- *Reading support* can be used alongside each source text so students can independently access an unseen text.
- *Preparing for writing* and *Preparing for reading* can be used to support students undertaking extended reading and writing tasks, particularly for the Putting it all together activities.
- *Reflection questions* can be used at any point during a lesson to delve further into students' thinking and identify where they can implement skills strategically.
- *Plan, monitor, evaluate* helps students to constructively approach the Putting it all together activities.
- *Learning log* can be used by students to summarise their learning at the end of every unit. This can be referred to for revision throughout students' KS3 learning.
- *Assessment wrapper* can be used alongside longer summative assessments to assess students' confidence, planning and self-regulation.
- *Self-regulation* can be used at the start of a task, unit or chapter to assess students' confidence and motivation.

Unit focus

Objectives

Students will:

- learn what is meant by rhetoric
- explore some key rhetorical devices
- use these devices to write and deliver a persuasive speech.

Unit texts

- 🔊 President Obama's victory speech, 2008
- **ⓚ** President Biden's inaugural speech, 2021 **WS**

Assessment

ⓚ 1.1 Mini-checkpoint quiz

Key terms

- **anecdote** a short or entertaining story about real people or events
- **emotive language** word choices that create a strong emotional reaction in the audience or reader
- **etymology** a description of the origin and history of a particular word
- **rhetorical device** a language feature that has a persuasive or impressive effect on listeners and readers
- **root** the core of a word that has meaning. It may or may not be a complete word

Introduction to the unit

Unit 1.1 *How do speakers use language to influence?* introduces the concept of power and rhetoric in persuasive discourse. Students will develop an understanding of what rhetoric is before identifying examples of rhetorical techniques in Barack Obama's victory speech and finally trying out these techniques for themselves. This knowledge-rich unit can be used to capitalise on the way that relevant topics of debate can fire students up. They will learn that they can harness the energy of their passions to good effect by engaging with the power of the English language and build their verbal skills to express themselves persuasively and with impact.

Activities

Starter activity

Ask students what it means to influence or be influenced. Is it a good or bad thing? How do we influence others, or how do they influence us? What sort of people influence you? This could lead to discussions about how different forms of media can influence positively or negatively and potentially to some sensitive topics around being influenced negatively to do something by peer pressure. Be aware of the scope for sensitive discussion topics and steer students to listen and share respectfully.

⚙ Activity 1

Students may draw on prior knowledge to identify language techniques and the impact of vocabulary choices. Ask students to make connections between texts they have encountered that use similar styles of language, e.g. speeches on television or in History lessons. Ask if audience and purpose are clearer in one example or another to draw out students' knowledge of register.

Kerboodle

The following activities can be replaced by the text and activities on 1.1 President Biden's inaugural speech worksheet.

Activity 2 Boosting your vocabulary

To support students to develop their understanding of root words, provide other examples and ask them to identify other variations, e.g. 'astro', 'bio', 'cardio'. To challenge more confident students to think more deeply about the words in part b, students could evaluate the importance of democracy/a democratic society. They could also consider the extent to which prosperity is important to them.

Activity 3 Building your knowledge

To ensure understanding of the rhetorical devices, particularly as parallelism and tricolon may be new terminology to students, ask them to write the definition in their own words. Check students' answers, perhaps asking them to explain how they know the technique is correctly identified to spot misconceptions. To extend this task ask students to explore what the impact is of using these techniques, making links to Obama's purpose.

Stretch yourself

Students may identify techniques such as anecdote, pronoun use, emotive language, repetition, etc. Encourage wider discussion about which rhetorical device is the most effective and why, drawing on factors such as sentence structure and use of punctuation for impact. For further stretch, explore word choices and semantic fields, and discuss the effects of more subtle techniques.

Activity 4 Building your knowledge

Aristotle's 'three appeals' are challenging but are broken down in manageable activities for students to work through. Students could discuss the activity as a class or in groups to then feed back to the class. To support less confident students, demonstrate the process of identifying one example before students identify the *logos* in Obama's speech.

Activity 5 Building your knowledge

Draw out prior knowledge of emotive language (e.g. from study of Malala Yousafzai's speech in Quest 1 Unit 1.8 *What's the right tone?*). Link this to *pathos* to make it clear that, although the concept sounds new, it is something students are familiar with. Use Activity 5b as an entry task to identifying emotive language before moving into Obama's speech. To extend this task, students could explore synonyms for Obama's emotive language choices and discuss the specific vocabulary choices made. For example: 'agony' or 'despair' could have been used instead of 'heartache'. Ask: *What are the connotations of each of these words? What is the impact on the reader?*

Activity 6 Building your knowledge

Remind students to use inference skills where values are not explicitly expressed. Model inference by verbalising the thought process behind it to help students who find this skill challenging, or scaffold this activity by providing a written prompt such as: 'The speaker values _____; this is shown when he says _____' to encourage students to identify a value and to evidence it from the text. To extend this task, students could consider the rhetorical technique of referring repeatedly to Ann Nixon Cooper to promote the speaker's *ethos*.

Activity 7 Putting it all together

This synoptic activity asks students to apply the techniques they have explored in Obama's speech to their own persuasive writing. Co-create success criteria with a focus on rhetorical devices. Consider model writing and explaining the choice of language and structure for the first paragraph (I do), then taking class feedback for paragraph 2 (we do), before handing over to the students (you do). Students should focus on the range of rhetorical devices they use and the vocabulary they choose to develop a clear tone and register for their writing. Ask students to perform their speeches and use peer assessment to identify the rhetorical techniques used and measure the effectiveness against success criteria.

Additional activities

Students could explore other famous speeches to identify use of the rhetorical devices they have studied. They could also identify the *logos*, *pathos* and *ethos* in speeches.

Unit focus

Objectives

Students will:

- learn how to provoke their audience into action
- explore structural techniques in a persuasive speech
- analyse the impact of a persuasive speech.

Unit texts

- ◁๑ Greta Thunberg's speech to the UK Parliament, 2019
- Ⓚ Megan Rapinoe's speech, 2019 **WS**

Assessment

- Ⓚ 1.2 Mini-checkpoint quiz

Key terms

- **antagonist** main opponent
- **antithesis** a rhetorical device that expresses opposing or contrasting ideas
- **direct address** addressing the reader as you
- **direct speech** the words that are actually spoken, usually presented in quotation marks
- **epigram** the expression of an idea in a short, memorable way
- **prefix** a word or group of letters placed in front of another word to add to or change its meaning
- **pronoun** a word used instead of a noun or noun phrase, e.g. *he, it, they*
- **superlative** the form of an adjective or adverb that means 'most'
- **tone** the speaker's (or writer's) feeling or attitude expressed towards their subject

Introduction to the unit

Unit 1.2 *How do speakers use structure to influence?* builds on the knowledge acquired in Unit 1.1 by continuing to explore how persuasive speeches are constructed. Focusing on an extract from a speech given by Greta Thunberg, students are encouraged to share their own opinions and critically evaluate both Thunberg's style and the extent to which she achieves her purpose of persuasion. Building on the foundation in Unit 1.1, students will continue to analyse rhetorical techniques while evolving their understanding of structural techniques to analyse impact in Thunberg's speech. Students will explore the use of direct speech and sentence structures, developing a deeper understanding of the writer's craft and the multiple interpretations different listeners and readers can have of one text.

Activities

Starter activity

Ask students to recall a time when someone said or posted online something that prompted them to do something they would not otherwise have done, e.g. sign a petition, donate to charity or make a purchase. Ask students to consider *why* what this person said made them want to make that change – was it because of who they were, or the way they said it, or both?

⚙ Activity 1

Activity 1 introduces the concept of epigrams and the term 'provoke'. Ask students to consider all possible meanings of 'provoke', e.g. 'influence', 'encourage', 'prompt', 'annoy', 'anger', 'motivate' and 'inspire'. Which meaning best fits the context of 'provoke your audience'? Ask whether provocation is a good or bad thing – explore different cases where speeches can be used to prompt good or bad outcomes. In part b, once students understand the epigram examples listed, discuss the purpose of the technique in persuasive writing.

Kerboodle

The following activities can be replaced by the text and activities on 1.2 Megan Rapinoe's 2019 speech worksheet.

⚙ Activity 2 Boosting your vocabulary

Draw on students' prior knowledge and cross-curricular experiences to connect the learning to the tier 3 vocabulary in the speech. Students could make links to Science and Geography and peer support may be useful in this activity. Students could also make connections between the use of tier 3 vocabulary in this speech and the concept of *ethos* (Unit 1.1) to explore to what extent Thunberg presents a positive *ethos* through her vocabulary choices.

Activity 3 Boosting your vocabulary

To ensure understanding of the term 'just' in this context, ask students for an example of a 'just' change that they have experienced, or an 'unjust' one! Discuss how understanding of prefixes can be used as a strategy to understand unfamiliar vocabulary in all of their learning.

It is possible student suggestions for Activity 3b will include 'transgender', 'transsexual', and 'transition' as gender reassignment. Ensure all discussions are sensitively managed, particularly if there are students in the class who may be directly affected by them.

Activity 4 Building your knowledge

Define 'tone' and ask students to give examples where they have either experienced or used a particular tone of voice and what the impact was. Read Thunberg's speech aloud to help students identify the tone. If students find this challenging, generate synonyms for tone and ask them to use these to complete a writing scaffold such as: 'Thunberg's tone is _____. This is shown when _____.' Remind students that tone is inferred from context.

⚙ Activity 5 Building your knowledge

Encourage students to draw on prior knowledge of pronoun use (Quest 1 Unit 2.3 *Who's telling the story?*). Check students' understanding of the tier 2 vocabulary listed by asking them to rank-order the emotive words from strongest to least strong, then to group the words by meaning, e.g: 'false', 'deceitful'

and 'dishonest' are all synonyms for one another, etc. Ask students to identify a piece of evidence for each group to identify the speaker's portrayal of different people. When it comes to writing out their responses, modelling 'I do, we do, you do' will support less confident students.

⚙ Activity 6 Building your knowledge

Introduce the key terms 'superlative' and 'antithesis' and give an example, such as Charles Dickens' opening line used in Activity 1 of Unit 1.1, 'It was the best of times, it was the worst of times'. Draw attention to the move of focus in this unit from language (Unit 1.1) to structure, in order to raise awareness of the skills they are developing. Students may feel more comfortable discussing the questions in pairs or groups and feeding back to the teacher as they get used to this shift.

Activity 7 Building your knowledge

To help students engage with the effect of using direct speech, ask them to read the lines in pairs, like a playscript conversation. Which speaker has more to say? Which speaker do they identify with, or feel more empathy with? What would the impact be if these points had been made without using dialogue?

⚙ Activity 8 Putting it all together

Like-minded peers could discuss their views in groups, then debate their ideas with an opposing view to rehearse their thoughts orally before writing their response. Co-create success criteria before students start writing, drawing out the need to identify relevant evidence from the text, as this is important for creating impact on the reader. Communicate to students the level of detail expected in their responses when analysing the impact of Thunberg's speech.

To challenge more confident students, ask them to compare Thunberg's speech with Obama's speech in Unit 1.1 and evaluate which they think is more persuasive.

Additional activities

There is a lot of new terminology in Units 1.1 and 1.2. Ask students to create a 'how to' guide for persuasive writing encompassing their learning so far which students can also use as a resource to support their learning in Unit 1.3.

Unit focus

Objectives
Students will:
- learn how to take part in a formal debate effectively
- practise the writing, speaking and listening skills needed for a debate
- participate in a formal debate in the classroom.

Unit text
- **k** 'To Eat or Not to Eat Meat' Gastropod **WS**

Assessment
k 1.3 Mini-checkpoint quiz

Key terms
- **chairperson** a person who is in charge of a meeting
- **counter-argument** an argument that opposes the point put forward
- **discourse marker** a word or phrase that makes a link between points and organises text
- **motion** a statement, idea or policy that is discussed in a debate
- **opposition** a statement that opposes a judgement or opinion
- **proposition** a statement that expresses a judgement or opinion
- **the floor** the formal term to describe everyone participating in a debate apart from the chairperson and main speakers
- **This house believes...** a formal way of introducing a motion

Introduction to the unit

Unit 1.3 *What is a debate?* challenges students to structure, prepare for and conduct a class debate. The focus in this unit is on developing a clearly structured argument and the activities guide students step-by-step to build their motion and prepare for counter-arguments. There is lots of subject terminology relating to formal debating, giving this unit a real connection to the outside world that it might be nice to connect to in school: extra-curricular clubs, career links and examples of actual parliamentary debates. There is an opportunity to teach and use discourse markers and activate and apply learning from Units 1.1 and 1.2 on rhetorical language and structural devices.

Activities

Starter activity
Explain to students that they will be taking part in a class debate in this unit. This may be a very daunting experience for students so sensitivity should be employed throughout the unit. Ask students how this task sits within their comfort zones and how they will motivate themselves or push themselves to contribute. To pre-empt Activity 1, discuss as a class how they can make each other feel comfortable and respected in this environment.

stimulate their existing knowledge, ask students to think about where they have seen debates in the past; what the difference is between debate and argument. Draw on past experiences of speaking and listening in other contexts, e.g. speeches or group work, and the skills they needed to be successful in these tasks. To engage students, show some video clips from formal debates and informal arguments to draw out what is and is not debate. This may help students to form some questions for the 'Find out' section of the table.

⚙ Activity 1
Students should draw on their prior knowledge to complete the 'Know' section of the KFL table. To

k Kerboodle
The following activities can be replaced by the text and activities on 1.3 'To Eat or Not to Eat Meat' worksheet.

⚙️ Activity 2 Building your knowledge

Begin by exploring the vocabulary of debate, e.g. 'motion', 'chairperson', 'proposition' and 'opposition'. Ask why a debate includes so much tier 3 vocabulary, bearing in mind the settings where formal debates take place. Activate students' prior knowledge from Unit 1.2 about the use of counter-arguments in persuasion, so they can apply these techniques to their own debate. To extend the activity, ask students to match arguments and counter-arguments and consider how they link.

Activity 3 Building your knowledge

This activity develops students' ability to structure an argument. To scaffold, use the 'Arguments for...' example from the Student Book to first demonstrate how rearranging the statements reduces impact – encourage students to explain why it is less impactful. In undertaking the 'Arguments against...' structuring independently, ask students to consider how their chosen order will impact the listeners and how it would change if they made different choices. Point out that all authors have to decide what information to reveal and when, so in analysing structure, we consider the choices the author has made – and therefore the decision students have made in this activity.

Activity 4 Building your knowledge

This activity challenges students to develop a more complex structure to their arguments. Use the example to generate success criteria for making well-developed points. Generate a shared writing board to record ideas for counter-arguments, facts and ideas for developing points, so they can refer to these when working independently.

Activity 5 Building your knowledge

In this activity students build their argument by using appropriate discourse markers to connect different points. Ask students to create a table using the headings listed in the teaching text above the activity – additional point, sequencing, counter-argument, effect, summarising – so that they can easily identify different types of discourse markers when writing their own. If more support is needed, provide a word bank with further types of discourse markers, or

direct students to use a thesaurus for synonyms of the examples given in the Student Book.

Stretch yourself

To extend this activity, ask students to consider discourse markers that create tone and add impact, e.g. adverbs such as 'allegedly', 'supposedly', 'undoubtedly', 'surprisingly'.

⚙️ Activity 6 Building your knowledge

This synoptic activity encourages students to utilise learning from previous units. They may need support with how to do this, e.g. by highlighting in their own work, or listing techniques and writing their own examples to check understanding.

Activity 7 Putting it all together

Students should ensure that as part of planning the debate, they are organising and structuring their ideas logically and using discourse markers to indicate to the listener how ideas are linked. Refer them back to page 27 of the Student Book for guidance on how to organise their ideas, develop detailed ideas and apply 'the ABC routine' in their planning and writing. Lastly, students should self-assess their work against the checklist created in Activity 6 to ensure they have used a wide range of rhetorical devices.

When it comes to performing the debate, introduce roles for students to increase accountability. For example, some students could be 'assessors' and feed back to the class at the end of the debate.

Ensure everyone is clear on their role and how they will contribute to the task. This accountability will also help them when returning to their KFL table.

⚙️ Additional activities

Give students the opportunity to explore how they would assess their own speaking and listening skills, e.g. success criteria which include volume, fluency and confidence as well as indications of listening, such as referencing something the previous person has said. More confident students could be challenged to create a 'how to' guide for conducting an effective debate, consolidating learning in this unit with their existing knowledge of effective speaking and listening skills.

Unit focus

Objectives

Students will:

- learn how dramatists present power through dialogue
- explore how vocabulary and sentence structure can reveal power and status
- write a dramatic scene, showing shifts of power between characters.

Unit text

- ◁》 *Noughts & Crosses* Malorie Blackman, dramatised by Dominic Cooke
- Ⓚ *The Crucible* Arthur Miller **WS**

Assessment

Ⓚ 1.4 Mini-checkpoint quiz; Chapter 1 Checkpoint 1 speaking and listening assessment; Chapter 1 Checkpoint 1 reading assessment

Key terms

- **connotation** an idea or feeling linked to a word, as well as its main meaning
- **declarative** a sentence that makes a statement
- **imperative** a sentence that gives an order, command or instruction
- **infer** to work something out from what is seen, said or done, even though it is not stated directly
- **interrogative** a sentence that asks a question
- **sarcasm** the use of humour or saying the opposite of what is meant to mock or criticise someone
- **synonym** a word or phrase that means the same, or almost the same, as another word or phrase

Introduction to the unit

Unit 1.4 *How do dramatists convey power?* prompts students to consider how power dynamics are at play in our lives and society, and how writers explore these dynamics through different means. Using an extract from a play, students will consider how the playwright creates shifts of power and status between characters through word choice, dialogue and structure. They will then apply these techniques in writing their own playscript.

The extract is taken from the playscript of *Noughts & Crosses,* which deals with issues of race. Make students aware of the sensitive nature of the topic and of their responsibility for the feelings and experiences of others in the room. Encourage students to draw on their understanding of the power of language and involve them in setting the parameters for respectful discussion throughout the lesson, including reaching a consensus about terminology that will be used to refer to race and related issues. Acknowledge that respectful listening is as important as respectful speaking.

Activities

✿ Starter activity

Activate prior knowledge by asking students what they know about playscripts and what conventions they expect to see in a playscript. They could share experiences of viewing theatre and explore why it can be challenging to analyse a playscript rather than prose (lack of description, need for inference, the importance of the performance, etc).

✿ Activity 1

Activity 1a is a good opportunity to draw on vocabulary choices and sentence types (interrogatives, imperatives, etc.). In 1b, encourage students to refer to all kinds of stories (not just fictional), making cross-curricular links with IT, PE and other areas where appropriate. Ask students to consider how it feels to be an audience to a power struggle (links to PSHE topics may be useful here) and who the audience most naturally feels empathy for and why. Activity 1c creates opportunity for enlightening conversations about sensitive topics relating to class, sexism and, potentially, racism. Be mindful of students' individual experiences and circumstances and ensure a sensitive and tactful approach – be prepared for the potential for strong opinions and remind students of respectful listening rules if necessary. Teachers could reactivate students' knowledge of power from Quest 1 – texts such as Wang Ping's poem about refugees 'Things We Carry on the Sea' (Unit 3.4) and Jacqueline Woodson's poems from *Brown Girl Dreaming* about experiencing racial segregation in the American South (Unit 3.8).

Ⓚ Kerboodle

The following activities can be replaced by the text and activities on 1.4 *The Crucible* worksheet.

Activity 2 Boosting your vocabulary

This activity explores the words in the extract that most pertinently represent power so that students can identify the power roles at play between the characters. Conduct a post-reading comprehension check to ensure students understand the action that is taking place in the extract.

Generate a word bank of synonyms and antonyms linked to power such as 'passive', 'submissive', 'subordinate', 'dominant' and 'commanding' to help students in their answers. Discuss how prefixes and suffixes can support their understanding of vocabulary, which will give them tools to understand texts independently in the future.

⚙ Activity 3 Building your knowledge

This activity asks students to identify power shifts between characters and how the author creates these shifts. Activate students' prior knowledge of the conventions of playwriting, such as the use of dialogue and stage directions, to consider the different techniques at play. Highlight to students that they will need to make inferences from what is written. To understand what is implied, students can take turns to play different characters and consider how the lines are delivered and how they feel saying them, or being on the receiving end of them, before they approach Activity 3b and 3c.

Activity 4 Building your knowledge

To support students, prompt them to consider the power plays that they experience themselves, both within their relationships with adults – family members, teachers, etc. – and within friendship groups. Ask whether they are happy for another to hold power, and how they would speak and behave if they wanted more power. To extend the activity, after completing Activity 4b, students could discuss their word choices and choice of punctuation to convey power and feed back their ideas as a class.

Activity 5 Putting it all together

In order to write a playscript that includes power shifts between characters, get students to apply what they have learned in Activities 3 and 4 about how writers show power, and then share these summaries to co-create success criteria for the task ahead. Students should aim to use declaratives, interrogatives and imperatives within dialogue to show power shifts. It might be helpful to model to students the difference between 'showing' and 'telling' so that students are implying power rather than explicitly stating it. An example could include a sentence such as 'I'm in charge now' (explicit – telling) compared to 'You will do as I tell you' (showing – implicit). Likewise, it may be helpful to explore how a writer can 'show' someone accepting the power dynamic – this could be done with stage directions as well as dialogue – so that students aren't just focusing on showing who has the power but also those who don't.

⚙ Additional activities

An additional opportunity for metacognitive reflection could be utilised here in which students explore their own motivation linked to power. They could consider how they feel when they do not hold power in school situations, e.g. being unsure what to do in a lesson, but being expected to complete the work set. How do they *want* to react? How *could* they react? How *should* they react? How can they help themselves to move away from how they *want* to react towards how they *should* react?

Students could refer back to their learning in Units 1.1 and 1.2 on rhetoric and consider how what they have learned in this unit links to their previous learning.

Unit focus

Objectives

Students will:

- learn how humour can influence readers' responses
- explore how sound patterns and structures convey the message of a poem
- write their own poem using a modelled structure.

Unit texts

- ◁)) 'Make Poetry Not War' Brian Bilston
- Ⓚ 'Warning' Jenny Joseph **WS**

Assessment

Ⓚ 1.5 Mini-checkpoint quiz

Key terms

- **quatrain** a stanza of four lines, often with a strict rhythm and rhyme scheme
- **rhyme** using the same sound to end words, particularly at the ends of lines
- **rhyming couplet** two consecutive lines of poetry that have rhyming final words
- **rhythm** the pattern of beats in a line of music or poetry

Introduction to the unit

Unit 1.5 *How is humour used in poetry?* looks closely at poetic form, building on the knowledge students will have obtained from Quest 1 Unit 1.2 *What is a poem?* Consider how best to introduce the challenging terms and concepts according to the particular needs of the class.

In this unit, students will begin by considering the power of words in society, and teachers should emphasise students' existing knowledge of language and power from the previous four units. They will then explore Bilston's poem 'Make Poetry Not War' by identifying how Bilston conveys a powerful message through humour, using sound patterns, language, poetic form, structure and rhyme. Students then write their own poem on a topic of their choice.

Activities

⚙ Starter activity

Ask students to discuss what they know and think about poetry. Encourage strong opinions and positive memories of experiencing poetry in primary school. Initiate a discussion about the usefulness of poetry – does it have a place in modern society? Does it have any power today? This will draw out students' knowledge of poetry and also increase confidence in talking about it in preparation for discussion of the poem in this unit.

⚙ Activity 1

Engage students by showing some video clips of powerful poetry (e.g. Prince EA) or comedians who make political points (e.g. Trevor Noah); the impact of satire could also be an interesting discussion topic. Ask students to consider how social media platforms give many people a voice to make a change.

Kerboodle

The following activities can be replaced by the text and activities on 1.5 'Warning' worksheet.

Activity 2 Boosting your vocabulary

To encourage less confident students, explain that the poem contains some challenging vocabulary, and ask them to read it alone the first time, noting any words that are new to them. Then read through the poem with the class, one stanza at a time. Discuss word choices and unfamiliar words as a group, tying in Activity 2a, 2b and 2c as students move though the poem.

Activity 3 Building your knowledge

Students could do this activity in pairs and feed back to the class to check their answers. Identify which, if any, of the techniques are new to students (e.g. consonance) and spend time exploring more examples of these.

Activity 4 Building your knowledge

This activity looks at imperatives and tone. Provide sentence starters or create a word bank of different words to describe 'tone' for Activity 4b to help students to write about their ideas in a structured way.

Activity 5 Building your knowledge

Students can read the poem aloud to determine the natural pace of the poem. Students could write out the poem using longer lines to see how the flow changes when read aloud. Lead a class discussion on which words have the most impact depending on whether they're read in short or long lines.

Activity 6 Building your knowledge

Encourage students to label each line of the poem with the rhyme scheme before they begin Activity 6. Some students may find it difficult to understand the impact of the rhyme scheme so consider displaying an 'alternative' version of the poem on the board where the last word has either been removed or changed so that it does not rhyme, to help them with their understanding to answer Activity 6a and 6b. In Activity 6c students generate some rhyming words that could be used in Bilston's poem. Encourage students to have fun exploring alternative rhyming words that do and do not work well in the context

and tone of the poem. For example, stupid/cupid could be an amusing juxtaposition in a poem about war, whereas using very violent imagery such as shot/hot or punch/crunch might change the tone of the poem, making it more serious and weakening the sense of humour within it. Before moving on to Activity 6d, ask students to evaluate the register and tone of the rhyming vocabulary to ensure they are maintaining the tone and style Bilston has created.

Activity 7 Putting it all together

Emphasise that this is a task students can have fun with, and experiment with language and redrafting. Encourage them to make annotations and edits to their own work. It may be helpful to ask students to consider their intentions – do they want their poem to amuse and entertain or do they want to convey a sense of anger about their topic within their poem? Once students have established their intentions and move on to Step 2, ask them to ensure their vocabulary choices and rhymes meet these intentions to help with tone and consistency in their writing. Scaffold the task by allowing students to work in small groups or pairs, providing them with a topic and some initial words in Step 1. Encourage pairs to swap work after each step so that they can support each other and add further ideas. If they feel comfortable doing so, ask students to read out their work and celebrate their identification of rhyming words, poetic form, consistent tone and use of humour.

Stretch yourself

This activity provides an opportunity for students to identify what is enjoyable about someone else's use of language, and to recognise the impact of their own language skills on another person. Encourage students to express what they find entertaining in each other's work and how this has been achieved through techniques.

Additional activities

Students could research contemporary spoken word poets and/or poetry slams and create their own spoken word poem to perform. They could explore the use of rap in the work of contemporary musicians such as Lin-Manuel Miranda and Ed Sheeran and explore how lyrics are also used to influence people.

Unit focus

Objectives
Students will:
- learn about the form and purpose of editorials
- explore techniques writers use to engage and persuade the reader
- comment on the effectiveness of a newspaper editorial.

Unit texts
- ◁)) 'Video games can improve mental health' Keza MacDonald
- ◁)) 'The Dartmoor wild camping ban further limits our right to roam' Sophie Pavelle
- 🄺 'Ultra-fast fashion is taking over' Zainab Mahmood **WS**

Assessment
🄺 1.6 Mini-checkpoint quiz

Key terms
- **antonym** a word that has the opposite meaning of a particular word
- **editorial** a newspaper article expressing a writer's opinion
- **the media** all means of communicating with a large audience through various outlets, such as television broadcasting, advertising, newspapers and the Internet

Introduction to the unit

Unit 1.6 *What is the power of the press?* encourages students to consider the extent to which editorial writing can influence the reader, building on their learning about persuasive writing and techniques in Quest 1 Unit 2.8 *Can a text change your mind?* and prior units in this chapter. Students will critically evaluate an editorial's use of rhetorical devices, facts and opinions to create impact and influence the reader. The activities increasingly challenge students, moving from identification of techniques to evaluation and analysis, supporting students to write confidently about the texts they encounter, and giving them confidence to form their own opinions.

Activities

Starter activity
Ask: *What is 'the press'?* Explore the multimedia approach the press can take, from newspapers and magazines to social media, TV and radio. Discuss how students engage with 'the press', how they think most people engage with it and how influential they think it is. Introduce the term 'editorial' as used in this context of journalism, which originally meant a text written as an opinion piece by the editorial team of the newspaper and was usually unnamed. However, the term is now used more flexibly, and can be applied to any article that is written as an opinion piece about current events.

⚙ Activity 1
Activate prior knowledge from Unit 1.3 in this activity and hold a mini-debate about the statements. Ask students to support their ideas with reasons, including anecdotes and facts. While students are speaking, ask other students to note the rhetorical techniques they use on the board, which will demonstrate the transferrable skills they're learning from across the units.

Kerboodle

The following activities can be replaced by the text and activities on 1.6 'Ultra-fast fashion is taking over' worksheet.

Activity 2

Encourage students to share their opinions, while drawing attention to the fact they are opinions, and highlight how fact and opinion are different to prepare for later activities. Remind students they don't have to have played or have an interest in video games to have an opinion on them, to ensure the discussion is inclusive.

Activity 3 Boosting your vocabulary

Ask students to link their knowledge of the words 'escapism', 'sinister' and 'insidious' to other nouns – what things are usually described by those words? This could lead to an exploration of connotation. Students could return to the text, identify other adjectives the author has used and group them into positive/negative to explore how descriptive words are used to create tone or an overall message within the article. Students should be familiar with using the Frayer model to explore words in depth following their work in Quest 1, but refer to the completed model for 'inspiring' in Unit 1.8 if helpful.

Activity 4 Building your knowledge

Ensure students understand the terminology in the introduction by showing them examples of different text types, such as a broadsheet newspaper, a celebrity magazine, articles on climate change. Check they correctly identify the purpose. Remind students of their prior learning of persuasive language techniques in Quest 1 Unit 2.8 *Can a text change your mind?* Ask students to verbalise the thought process behind their decision-making (the evidence found, and what they can infer, etc.) to support them in completing Activity 4 independently.

Activity 5 Building your knowledge

Remind students of the skills of skimming and scanning and model this by working through the first paragraph as a class to support them in locating and identifying facts, statistics and emotive language. Students can then work independently on the rest of the text before discussing their answers as a class.

Activity 6 Building your knowledge

Refresh students' memories of rhetorical language and devices covered in Units 1.1 and 1.2. For Activity 6b, using the model answer ask students to generate success criteria to help plan their paragraph and self-assess their work.

Activity 7 Building your knowledge

Ask students to discuss this activity in pairs/small groups and to listen to others' ideas and responses. Hold a class vote as to whether or not students' minds were changed. Pose the question: *What could the author have done differently to persuade you more?* to lead to a consideration of techniques and content they could apply to their own writing.

Activity 8 Putting it all together

Read the extract as a class and identify the purpose of the text and the writer's perspective. To increase student confidence in approaching the text independently, generate a class discussion around to what extent students agree or disagree with the writer's perspective, or to what extent they think the text is engaging and how well it influences the reader. First, students could make a note of the key words in the question, then identify examples of the techniques listed in the bullet points within the extract, before finally considering the impact of the techniques on the reader. For less confident students, co-create a word bank and some sentence starters for each bullet point. To increase the level of challenge, provide success criteria that focus specifically on developing more detailed analysis, e.g. identifying more subtle techniques such as exploring word connotation.

Additional activities

Students could write their own editorials on issues relevant to school life for a class newspaper, choosing from one of the four types: news-focused, celebratory, critical or persuasive.

1.7 How do adverts persuade people?

Student Book pp 48–53

Unit focus

Objectives

Students will:

- learn how visual advertisements attract attention and influence people
- explore how symbols, slogans and rhetorical devices can convey powerful messages simply
- write an advertisement to influence people's behaviour.

Unit texts

- ◁◦ Poster 1 'Catch it. Bin it. Kill it.'
- ◁◦ Poster 2 'Coughs and sneezes spread diseases'
- ◁◦ Poster 3 'Don't let thieves shatter your Christmas'
- Ⓚ This Girl Can campaign poster **WS**

Assessment

Ⓚ 1.7 Mini-checkpoint quiz

Key terms

- **multimodal** having or involving many methods (modes), e.g. text, images, motion, audio
- **slogan** a short, catchy word or phrase used to advertise something or represent the aims of a campaign or organisation
- **summarise** to give the key points
- **symbol** something specific that represents a more general quality or situation
- **tricolon** a pattern of three words or phrases grouped together to be memorable and have impact

Introduction to the unit

Unit 1.7 *How do adverts persuade people?* introduces students to multimodal texts, in particular the form of print and online advertisements. Students will explore how language, combined with imagery, can have a powerful impact on an audience. The unit asks students to consider the role adverts play in their own lives, to analyse the use of images, symbols and slogans in texts and then to apply this knowledge by creating their own adverts. New terminology such as 'slogan' and 'symbol' is introduced which students will need explicitly teaching before undertaking the Building your knowledge section.

Activities

Starter activity

Remind students that this chapter is called 'Power and influence'. In relation to this title, what roles do power and influence play in advertising? The question: *To what extent do you think advertising has power and influence over you?* could spark an engaging discussion about the potential benefits and harms of advertising.

⚙ Activity 1

Students could walk around the school, noting the types of advertising they see and the form and purpose of each example. Ask them to consider the number of adverts linked to different issues, e.g. uniform, school mottoes, events, well-being, etc. Discuss why there are more of some than others, and where they are placed and why.

Ⓚ Kerboodle

The following activities can be replaced by the text and activities on 1.7 This Girl Can worksheet.

⚙ Activity 2

Direct students to key aspects of the posters, e.g. the images, fonts, use of colour, language. Discuss how each of these gives clues about when the text was created, and show students that this process is a useful means of approaching unseen texts in future. Encourage students to draw on their prior knowledge of social and historical change, and how the different contexts influence the two posters.

Activity 3 Boosting your vocabulary

Extend the discussion around Activity 3a by exploring why authors might have to plan for readers not reading the text in full and how this impacts design choices, tying in the origin of the word 'advert' in 3b.

Activity 4 Building your knowledge

This could be a timed activity to encourage students to make notes efficiently. Extend the activity by asking students to convey a specific message through symbols or emojis (e.g. 'do your homework'). How challenging is it? How effective? Explore how and why images and words used together have the most impact.

⚙ Activity 5 Building your knowledge

Remind students of their work in Unit 1.1 on rhetorical devices to support them in their answers. To extend this task ask students to evaluate how effective the advert is in communicating its message – ask students what action they would take as a result of seeing this advert or what would make the advert more effective.

Stretch yourself

Students could consider the tone they wish to create through their tricolon, e.g. authoritative or emotive. Ask students to justify their choices linked to the advert's purpose.

⚙ Activity 6 Building your knowledge

Students can work in small groups or pairs to write their analytical responses considering the impact of rhetorical devices identified. Alternatively, teachers could model an answer verbalising the 'expert' thought process and ask students to identify sentence starters and/or success criteria to support them to make appropriately detailed meaningful responses.

⚙ Activity 7 Building your knowledge

Once students have created their slogan, ask them to apply the principles from Activity 6b to a peer's work – they will need identify the rhetorical devices used and analyse the impact. To challenge students, ask them to write alternative versions to their main slogan, e.g. by changing a word or using a different rhetorical device; they can explain in each case the impact the chosen language and rhetorical device have on the power of the message.

⚙ Activity 8 Putting it all together

Remind students of what they learned in Activity 6 about rhetorical devices and the effects they can have on readers. Encourage students to consider the connotations of visual symbols and colours, as well as vocabulary choices.

Students could peer assess each other's work, annotating it with the connotations and rhetorical techniques they can identify, then grading it against a scale from 1 to 10, with 10 being 'I will follow this advert's instruction' and 1 being 'I don't believe this advert'. Ask students to justify their rating against the success criteria.

Additional activities

For homework or using IT resources in school, students could collate a number of adverts for the same product or idea, then rank them in order of effectiveness. Ask them to explain their ranking with reference to use of language devices, slogans, colours, images, etc.

Unit focus

Objectives

Students will:

- learn how informal language can influence some audiences
- explore the use of non-standard English, including abbreviations and colloquial expressions
- comment on the language used in an article about teenage influencers.

Unit texts

- 🔊 'Teen Influencers Showing Us How It's Done' Nicole P. Dunford
- 🔊 'Best Teenager Influencers' Bonita Brown
- Ⓚ 'How to have your best April' Purely Ella **WS**

Assessment

Ⓚ 1.8 Mini-checkpoint quiz; Chapter 1 Checkpoint 2 writing assessment; Chapter 1 Checkpoint 2 reading assessment

Key terms

- **abbreviation** a shortened form of a word or phrase
- **colloquial** suitable for ordinary conversation rather than formal speech or writing
- **exclamatory statement** a sentence that expresses sudden or strong emotions, such as excitement. It usually ends with an exclamation mark
- **non-standard English** an informal version of English, often used with family and friends, including slang and regional variations
- **second person** a narrative voice that addresses the reader directly, using the pronoun 'you'
- **Standard English** a widely recognised, formal version of English, not linked to any region, but used in schools, exams, official publications and in public announcements

Introduction to the unit

Unit 1.8 *How does informal language influence others?* is a great opportunity to capitalise on students' knowledge and experience of influencers and celebrate their passion for the subject. Students will first have a chance to share their culture and experiences of being influenced by others, which leads to a valuable opportunity to embrace their identity in the classroom. After sharing their experiences, students will look at a text aimed at businesses and teenagers and explore how language and register work together to influence the reader. Students will identify colloquial and non-standard English and consider the impact of non-standard English, before analysing language techniques more broadly in writing tasks. This unit combines many of the techniques and principles learned in previous units such as the trustworthiness of a speaker (Unit 1.1) and the language of power in sentence types (Unit 1.4).

Activities

⚙ Starter activity

To hook students' interest, display photos or invite suggestions of a range of influencers, from historical figures such as Emmeline Pankhurst and Rosa Parks, through to online influencers who are popular with students today. Encourage cross-curriculum knowledge from History, Politics, Science, Art, etc. Ask students to rate the level of influence of each person on society. This could lead to a meaningful discussion around the responsibility influencers hold.

⚙ Activity 1

To extend this activity, ask students who they think should influence them. This could open up an interesting and potentially sensitive discussion around peer pressure. Discuss the importance of recognising when you're being influenced by others for the wrong reasons and/or the impact of the idea of punishment or consequence. Does this influence their actions? In 1c, discuss the impact of language choices such as modal verbs, or sentence types such as imperatives.

Ⓚ Kerboodle

The following activities can be replaced by the text and activities on 1.8 'How to have your best April' worksheet.

Activity 2 Boosting your vocabulary

To encourage detailed and considered responses to Activity 2a ii, model 'thinking aloud' about the connotations of some of the synonyms. Encourage students to use a dictionary for the characteristics box for the Frayer model in 2b. To extend, students could make a list of synonyms as well as antonyms for 'unique' and come up with two or three example sentences.

Activity 3 Building your knowledge

This is an engaging activity where students can be encouraged to share the abbreviations they use in their daily lives with their friends and family and ask them to consider if they are easily understood or need explaining. Students could explore why teenagers have so many abbreviations that are non-standard English – how does this distinguish them from adults? Why might they want a degree of separation through language?

⚙ Activity 4 Building your knowledge

Remind students of their learning about non-standard English and tone in Quest 1 Units 1.7 *Which English do you speak?* and 1.8 *What's the right tone?* Point out that this activity builds on that knowledge. This is a helpful time to draw attention to the need for a consistent register in writing. Ask: *If the writer had used a mixture of Standard and non-standard English, what would the impact be?* A consistent register is something that can be challenging for students to maintain while writing, so discuss ways of remembering audience and purpose, checking register and tone.

⚙ Activities 5 and 6 Building your knowledge

These tasks build the knowledge and skills students will need for analysing language in Activity 7. Use the 'I do, we do, you do' approach so that Activity 5b is teacher-modelled, the class works on Activity 6b together, then students approach Activity 7 independently. For Activity 5b, model the thought process of writing a response to a text by explicitly verbalising the reason for choosing the two techniques, how they impact the reader and how the techniques support the purpose and intentions of the text. Students can then identify key words or sentence starters which they can utilise in their own work for the following activities. Activity 6a is an opportunity to discuss audience perceptions of non-standard English. Encourage a respectful approach towards different variations of non-standard English depending on culture and locality; emphasise that they are all valid and valuable. Create a list of 'rules' as to when non-standard English can be used. Direct students to focus on purpose, audience and the author's intentions, then use the responses to Activities 5 and 6 to create success criteria for Activity 7.

Activity 7 Putting it all together

Divide the bullet points across the class so students can work in pairs or small groups on one bullet point then feed back to the class, who can add to their own individual notes to inform their final written response; correct any misconceptions. Suggest to students that the author may have more than one intention or purpose for the text. The class could generate a number of intentions and/or purposes and rank order them from most to least important or obvious, etc. Students may need further support in identifying the abbreviations and colloquialisms and identifying how these impact the tone of the writing and support the writer's purpose. It may be helpful to generate a word bank, considering the different effects of techniques on the reader.

Additional activities

Students could create an 'Adult's guide to non-standard English cheat sheet' which includes students' everyday abbreviations and colloquialisms with definitions. Referring to the learning journey in the Student Book, students could bring together all of their learning from across the chapter and complete the Kerboodle resource *Post-chapter reflection*.

② Terror and wonder

  Chapter overview

In this chapter students will have the opportunity to explore the concepts of terror and wonder through a range of fiction and non-fiction texts, spanning topics from vampires and ghosts to artificial intelligence and space. Units 1–4 take students on a journey through gothic fiction, exploring genre conventions, the subversion of conventions, the creation of tension, and gothic settings. Students will deep dive into how authors use figurative language to impact the reader by exploring language techniques such as metaphor, symbolism and juxtaposition and structural techniques to encourage a deeper understanding of how writers' choices influence readers. Students will use their knowledge of language and structural techniques to develop analytical responses to reading, and apply this knowledge to their own writing. In Units 5–8, students will encounter instructional texts, news articles and autobiography. Students will develop their knowledge of how writers vary their use of language and structure to suit audience, purpose and form. They will explore the impact of word choice, figurative language and register, and consider the context of texts on the writer's attitude and viewpoint. Students will compare how writers present viewpoint in two texts and create their own instructional and autobiographical writing.

This chapter builds on Quest 1 and the Year 7 curriculum by increasing the depth of understanding about how texts are deliberately crafted and constructed for impact. There is ample opportunity to activate prior knowledge from Quest 1 and the teacher guidance signposts the opportunities to do so. There is an increase in the level of challenge in tasks, both in the depth of thinking required and in the subject terminology that students will encounter, but tasks are sequenced effectively to encourage learner independence. Opportunities for metacognition to further support learner independence are also signposted in the teacher guidance alongside creative and collaborative learning opportunities to foster the joy of learning.

  **Texts**

The texts in this chapter have been chosen to provide a range of diverse and engaging reading experiences for students. Students may recognise extracts from contemporary gothic texts such as *Twilight* but will also enjoy the opportunity to engage with literary heritage texts such as H. G. Wells' 'The Red Room' and Shakespeare's *Hamlet*. The non-fiction texts featured in Units 5–8 consider contemporary topics, allowing students to engage with topics that are relevant to our ever-changing society and can make links to their own lived experience.

Discussions around sexism, technological safeguarding and the supernatural may be inspired by the texts in this chapter. Encourage students to share their opinions respectfully and sensitively, accepting the views of others even if they differ from their own.

Key

 Kerboodle

 Audio

 Reading skill

 Writing skill

 Speaking and listening skill

WS Worksheet

2A Terror and wonder

Unit	Texts	Objectives
1 What is gothic fiction?	• ◁» 'The Red Room' H. G. Wells • ◁» *Dracula* Bram Stoker • Ⓚ *Jane Eyre* Charlotte Brontë **WS**	• Learn about the genre of gothic fiction • Explore how writers use the conventions of gothic fiction • Comment on the use of gothic conventions in a text
2 How can a setting create fear?	• ◁» *Fog Island* Mariette Lindstein • Ⓚ *The Haunting of Hill House* Shirley Jackson **WS**	• Learn how writers create sinister settings • Explore the use of language and structural techniques to build fear and tension • Write the opening of a story describing a sinister setting
3 How do writers subvert a genre?	• ◁» *Twilight* Stephenie Meyer • ◁» *A Monster Calls* Patrick Ness • Ⓚ *Good Boy* Mal Peet **WS**	• Learn how writers subvert and adapt genres over time • Explore the use of gothic conventions in contemporary stories • Comment on how a writer subverts gothic conventions to create fear and tension
4 How is figurative language used to create fear?	• ◁» *Hamlet* William Shakespeare • Ⓚ *Richard III* William Shakespeare **WS**	• Learn how dramatists use language to control the reaction of their audience • Explore how figurative language, including imagery, can create fear and tension • Write and present a dramatic speech for a ghostly character

Checkpoint Assessment: Chapter 2 Checkpoint 1 reading assessment; Chapter 2 Checkpoint 1 writing assessment

2B Terror and wonder

Unit	Texts	Objectives
5 How do writers guide their readers?	• ◁» 'An astronomer's guide to stargazing' Mary McIntyre • Ⓚ 'How to Set Up Your Smart Home' John R. Delaney and Whitson Gordon **WS**	• learn how a guide can combine instructions and advice • explore how the structure and language features of a guide help to fulfil its purpose • write a guide of their own, including instructions and advice
6 How do writers provide explanation?	• ◁» 'The Environmental Benefits of Driverless Cars' Ashleigh Rose-Harman • Ⓚ 'Five ways AI is saving wildlife' Graeme Green **WS**	• learn about explanation texts and their conventions • explore the effects of structure and language features in an explanation text • comment on how a writer uses the features of an explanation text in an article
7 How do we compare texts?	• ◁» 'Meet the one-eyed robot – it's fantastic' Nicholas Lloyd • ◁» 'Helping companies deploy AI models more responsibly' Zach Winn • Ⓚ 'You'll Be Able To Carry Phone' **WS** • Ⓚ 'Best smartphone 2023' Chris Rowlands **WS**	• learn how to structure a comparison of two texts • explore how writers' choice of language and register is shaped by purpose, audience and context • compare two texts written on a similar topic
8 How do writers present themselves?	• ◁» *My Remarkable Journey: A Memoir* Katherine Johnson • Ⓚ *Limitless: The Autobiography* Tim Peake **WS**	• learn how an autobiography can inform and entertain a reader • explore the conventions of autobiographies • write an extract from your own autobiography about something you have done

Checkpoint Assessment: Chapter 2 Checkpoint 2 reading assessment; Chapter 2 Checkpoint 2 writing assessment

Background knowledge

Terror and wonder is a broad topic that could encompass any number of subtopics. The issues broached in this chapter celebrate a literary heritage in which fears can be safely explored through stories. Although gothic (arguably) began with Horace Walpole's *The Castle of Otranto* in 1764, gothic conventions have been around for much longer – exemplified by the ghost in *Hamlet*. From this, the genre grew in popularity during the Georgian and Victorian eras. Gothic fiction was used as a way to explore the very real fears the fast-changing Industrial Revolution society was experiencing, through novels such as Mary Shelley's *Frankenstein* and Robert Louis Stevenson's *Jekyll and Hyde*. The characters and settings in fiction formed a useful façade through which to explore much broader issues, such as technology. Units 5–8 explore the future of technology our own society faces: from driverless cars to the potential of AI robots and the unknown universe beyond our planet.

To make this relevance explicit to students, discuss their fears about technology, how it can help them, but how it can also be a hindrance to their well-being (social media addiction, for example). Students may not be aware of the literary heritage that precedes the science fiction of today, or of how closely fiction is linked to reality or how it is utilised to help us make sense of reality. Lastly, draw on students' prior experience and knowledge of the theme of terror and wonder in fictional texts they may have studied in KS2, such as *Moondial* by Helen Cresswell.

Cross-curricular links

The selected texts link with several other areas of the curriculum, particularly History, such as Katherine Johnson's autobiography that addresses the discrimination she experienced due to her race and sex. In Units 2.6 and 2.7 modern technology is explored, which links to KS3 Science and IT. Issues such as isolation, religion and the supernatural are evident in the fiction texts written by Stephenie Meyer, Shakespeare and H.G. Wells; these topics are relevant to aspects of the citizenship/PSHE curriculum and to Religious Studies. Use these links to draw on students' wider knowledge of, or relevant connections to, the topic to help deepen their understanding of the issues presented.

Representation and inclusion

The broad range of texts aims to foster a sense of self-confidence and self-esteem as students see aspects of themselves, their peers or their experiences represented in writing. Many of the units encourage students to develop a personal opinion on topics and the texts read, as well as offering opportunities to share their own experiences and celebrate what makes them unique.

Texts such as Stephenie Meyer's *Twilight* portray the sense of frustration and helplessness lots of young people feel as they move towards maturity and yearn for independence and more control over their own lives. Hamlet's exploration of his relationship with a parental figure is also a key experience students may relate to.

It is worth noting that historic texts often use tropes that are now problematic; the gothic convention of evil being represented by 'frightening', 'monstrous' characters with 'grotesque' physical features is built on outdated ideas about disabled people or those with physical differences as objects of fear. These portrayals dehumanised those with visible differences and who were disabled. Be alert and sensitive to this, and discuss how such conventions reflect attitudes of their cultural context.

The chapter includes several articles on technology in our future. Encourage students to make predictions and hypothesise about their own experiences of and reactions to future technology, to celebrate the unknown rather than fear it and to consider their own career options in light of the society of tomorrow.

🄚 Kerboodle texts

Several alternative routes are offered on Kerboodle, so students can follow the same learning objectives in each unit while focusing on text choices that best suit their ability profile or interests. The texts range across several centuries, reflecting both male and female perspectives, as well as different cultural views, including novels such as Charlotte Brontë's *Jane Eyre* and Mal Peet's *Good Boy*, Shakespeare's *Richard III,* articles on modern technology, as well as Tim Peake's autobiography *Limitless*.

💬 Assessment

Mini-checkpoint quizzes, with automatic next steps built in, can be completed by students after each unit.

Spelling, punctuation and grammar mini-checkpoint quizzes can also be completed after every two units. These quizzes can be used to reinforce learning that students acquired in Year 7 or be used to support any spelling, punctuation and grammar lessons that are being undertaken in Year 8.

Checkpoint assessments are available to students after every fourth unit, after each part of the chapter. These assess students' knowledge, and skills are based on the core skills in the Quest assessment levels. Students can use the *Assessment wrapper* resource on Kerboodle while undertaking these assessments, which comprises a pre-assessment and post-assessment reflection exercise to help plan and review what they have learned.

☆ Further reading

The books and playscript below will complement the units in Chapter 2 and could be used in whole-class reading, as a class reader or in a drama session.

The Rollercoaster titles have online resource packs that will be useful when planning.

Rollercoaster *Sawbones* Catherine Johnson
Super-Readable Rollercoaster *Dark Peak* Marcus Sedgwick
Oxford Playscripts *Flesh and Blood* Benjamin Hulme-Cross

Chapter opener

⚡ How to use the chapter opener

The chapter opener includes an introduction to the units with some questions to prompt students to think about the topic and to recall prior learning. The chapter opener will help prepare students in understanding the texts covered in the units. It can be used to initiate a discussion about what content students think might be covered in the chapter and to explore any background knowledge they have, or might need to have. It can also be used to help students review their understanding at the end of the chapter and discuss what they have learned.

Ask students to define the terms 'terror' and 'wonder' and consider connotations of the words. Ask: *Can 'terror' be interchanged with 'wonder' or 'excitement'? Is terror always a bad thing?* Alternatively, students could predict the sorts of texts and topics they may encounter in this chapter.

Students could consider their own experiences of encountering something scary or awesome and break down the multiple feelings that are included in the concept of fear or awe. Explore whether students want to be scared and why/why not. Discuss films or books they have enjoyed that have induced fear.

Introduce students to the literary heritage of gothic fiction from Georgian England to the present day and discuss why the genre has been so popular. Drawing out typical gothic conventions will be useful for Unit 1.

Explore why the topics of space and technology appear in a chapter on terror and wonder. Why and at what points in history has technology been something to fear? Ask: *Is technology feared now?* Invite students to share existing knowledge of space and/or generate questions they have about the future of technology and space connected to ideas of terror and wonder.

Create a vocabulary crib sheet with synonyms for feelings of fear to provide students with a bank of vocabulary to utilise in their work in Chapter 2.

Ask students to complete the start of unit reflection to activate their knowledge of the skills they have and will need in this unit.

Introduce students to a number of images (in addition to those in the Student Book) to stimulate and support this discussion. This could be images of gothic settings, aliens, supernatural creatures, etc. or film posters/front covers of novels and news headlines linked to the topics students will encounter in this unit.

Students could create a vocabulary bank to support their responses to images. Introduce a list of 'banned' words such as 'scared' or 'confused' to ensure varied and thoughtful responses.

Remind students of the features of a blurb or ask them to generate the list of features they would need to include in a blurb, e.g. rhetorical questions, a cliff-hanger, ellipses, etc. Students could then annotate the features with their intended reader reaction, e.g. cliff-hanger to create a sense of intrigue, ellipsis to create tension, etc.

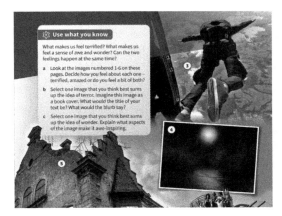

Consider the etymology of the words 'awe' and 'wonder'. Does one word suggest more power or hold more gravitas than the other? Why? Explore words that induce feelings of awe, for example: feats of human endurance or power, nature, human-built structures, etc. Students could try to rank different 'awe-inspiring' experiences on a scale from 'wonder' to 'awe', applying a different synonym increasing in intensity to each experience.

 ## Key vocabulary

The vocabulary introduced in the chapter opener forms the basis for the subsequent topics in the Student Book. These specialist items of terminology are building blocks for students to become familiar with and to begin to use with confidence in response to texts.

Students will have met much of this vocabulary during KS2 and their first year of KS3. However, some students may struggle to visualise the more abstract concepts. Visual reminders on classroom wall displays may help, as well as providing definitions to reinforce the meanings.

Explore the chapter's key words through activities:

1 Use Frayer diagrams to explore these words.
2 Find images to go with each word.
3 Use each word in a sentence.
4 Explore the morphology of some words. For example, what does the prefix 'sub' reveal about the word?
5 Consider which words students have come across before and ask them to rank order them by confidence in their understanding of the word. Predict how this knowledge will help in this unit.
6 Link the words: students could make a flow diagram or mind map using arrows to make connections between the words, considering synonyms or antonyms and relation by definition or word class, etc.

Words you need to know

awe, wonder, genre, conventions, typical, atypical, subversion, supernatural

Learning overview

The learning overview provides students with a unit-by-unit breakdown of what to expect in the chapter. The aim of the learning overview is to:

- activate prior knowledge
- demonstrate the sequential learning that students will undertake so they can make connections between their learning from one unit to the next
- illustrate the bigger picture of what students will learn so they understand how each unit builds their knowledge and skills to succeed in the English curriculum, and so they can apply knowledge to the real world
- give students the opportunity to practise self-regulation in the face of new learning by considering motivation and how to approach potential challenges in the units ahead.

Each box within the learning overview asks students a question (Prepare) to help them activate their prior learning for that unit before explaining the 'what' and the 'how': what students can expect to learn in the unit (What I will learn) and the tasks they can expect to complete (How I will learn). Each chapter's unique learning overview provides prompts and mini-activities to encourage and engage students ahead of the primary work.

2.1 How I will learn: Ask students to name genres they are aware of. Can they identify any conventions of different genres? What can students remember about how to write an analysis? Link the reading tasks to the demands of GCSE so students understand the transferability of the tasks.

2.3 Prepare: Students should consider what it means if something is 'familiar'. They could explore the connotations of the word before they discuss the prompt question. They could activate prior knowledge from Unit 2.2 when they explored what makes a setting scary and contrast this against the idea of the familiar.

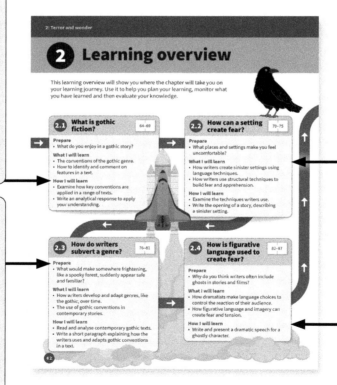

2.2 What I will learn: Ask students: *What is a setting?* Prompt them to discuss any settings they have read about or seen in films that were particularly memorable because they were scary. Ask students to share their ideas and consider the follow-up questions: *Do they have anything in common? What makes a place scary?*

2.4 How I will learn: Ask students to consider their motivation levels at the thought of writing a dramatic speech for a ghostly character. They could activate their prior knowledge of dramatic writing conventions and/or consider the challenges they face when asked to write creatively and how to overcome these.

2.5 How I will learn: Ask students to define the difference between 'instructions', 'advice' and 'guidance'. Ask students to consider who might deliver each type of information, but also who they might ask for each type and when/why. They should give examples.

2.7 What I will learn: Ask what students hope they will learn before they complete this task. Generate a list of their questions and expectations and refer to this throughout the unit. They can write anonymous questions or concerns about completing this task which can be used to inform planning.

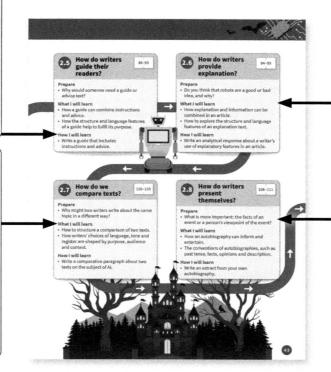

2.6 What I will learn: Ask students to explain the difference between informing and explaining. Is there much difference? Why/why not? Students could predict what skills they already have that they might need to use in the unit and what prior knowledge might help them.

2.8 Prepare: Draw attention to text purpose and audience. Possible supplementary questions include: *When would a purely factual account be appropriate? When are opinions necessary? Which is most entertaining? Why?*

⚙ Metacognition

The activities in each chapter set out to make the implicit, explicit: to draw out what many students will already intuitively know but not necessarily be aware of knowing.

On Kerboodle, metacognitive resources are available to use alongside teaching and to support students throughout the chapter and while completing activities.

- *Pre-chapter reflection* supports students to engage with the content within the chapter opener and learning overview.
- *Post-chapter reflection* supports students at the end of chapters to reflect on and consolidate their learning.
- *Reading support* can be used alongside each source text so students can independently access an unseen text.
- *Preparing for writing* and *Preparing for reading* can be used to support students undertaking extended reading and writing tasks, particularly for the Putting it all together activities.
- *Reflection questions* can be used at any point during a lesson to delve further into students' thinking and identify where they can implement skills strategically.
- *Plan, monitor, evaluate* helps students to constructively approach the Putting it all together activities.
- *Learning log* can be used by students to summarise their learning at the end of every unit. This can be referred to for revision throughout students' KS3 learning.
- *Assessment wrapper* can be used alongside longer summative assessments to assess students' confidence, planning and self-regulation.
- *Self-regulation* can be used at the start of a task, unit or chapter to assess students' confidence and motivation.

Unit focus

Objectives

Students will:

- learn about the genre of gothic fiction
- explore how writers use the conventions of gothic fiction
- comment on the use of gothic conventions in a text.

Unit texts

- ◁ » 'The Red Room' H. G. Wells
- ◁ » *Dracula* Bram Stoker
- Ⓚ *Jane Eyre* Charlotte Brontë **WS**

Assessment

Ⓚ 2.1 Mini-checkpoint quiz

Key terms

- **convention** a typical feature you find in a particular genre
- **genre** a type of story, e.g. *horror, romance, adventure, science fiction*
- **narrator** a person who tells a story, especially in a book, play or film
- **symbol** something specific that represents a more general quality or situation
- **synonym** a word or phrase that means the same, or almost the same, as another word or phrase
- **tension** a feeling of being on edge with nerves stretched tight
- **the supernatural** events and forces that cannot be explained by the known laws of nature or science

Introduction to the unit

Unit 2.1 *What is gothic fiction?* introduces students to the key conventions of gothic fiction using two extracts taken from famous gothic texts: H. G. Wells' 'The Red Room' and Bram Stoker's *Dracula*. Students will draw on prior knowledge of genre and conventions and extend this knowledge by exploring the conventions specific to gothic fiction, including unnerving characters and isolated settings, and techniques such as symbolism and the creation of tension.

Students may benefit from activating hinterland knowledge of Victorian writing and historical context to develop deeper understanding of the genre and its popularity. Students will continue to develop their analysis skills by completing activities that lead to a final task of independently analysing how gothic conventions are used to create mystery and fear in the extract from *Dracula*. This activity increases in the level of challenge from a scaffolded approach to 'The Red Room' to an independent approach to *Dracula*.

Activities

✿ Starter activity

To engage students with the concept of genre conventions and draw on prior knowledge from past Quest units, show examples of different genres and ask students to identify the genre and recall different conventions. For example: a picture of Sherlock Holmes or a still from *The Hobbit* to draw out knowledge of conventions of crime fiction and quest stories, etc. As they read the teaching texts in the Student Book, ask students to make their own notes about the different conventions of gothic fiction that they are learning. This will prepare and support them for the final activity.

✿ Activity 1

To begin developing understanding of the types of vocabulary they will encounter, students could annotate a copy of the picture with descriptive language and the language devices they might use to create a spooky mood. Discuss how their chosen words and techniques link to what they would expect to see in gothic fiction, drawing on their knowledge of other gothic texts and media. For Activity 1b activate students' prior knowledge of genre from films/books such as *The Woman in Black, Frozen*

Charlotte and/or TV series such as *Stranger Things*. It may be helpful to explore the distinction between gothic and horror at this point.

🅚 Kerboodle
The following activities can be replaced by the text and activities on 2.1 *Jane Eyre* worksheet.

Activity 2 Boosting your vocabulary
Ask students to identify the vocabulary in the extract that they think links to the 'spectral' presence to consider more widely how an eerie atmosphere has been created using the senses. This could lead to a discussion around semantic fields or an exploration of connotation. Students could also create a list of antonyms to contrast with these ideas to explore how a different word choice can transform the atmosphere created within a text.

Activity 3 Building your knowledge
Ask students to complete a Frayer model on the word 'haunted' to help them answer Activity 3a. Direct students to consider the use of punctuation when exploring the response of the old man and woman in 3b, as well as the use of verbs such as 'jerked', 'staggered' and 'staring'.

Activity 4 Building your knowledge
Ask students to draw the characters and label their drawings with key quotations from the text that signify unusual aspects of their appearance and behaviour. Discuss with students how these create a sense of uncertainty and fear, linking back to gothic conventions.

⚙ Activity 5 Building your knowledge
Before identifying examples of 'light' and 'dark' in the text, mind map connotations of the two terms and consider the meaning behind the symbolism. Draw students' attention to the author's use of contrast and explore the impact of this: how the two choices available to the narrator are used to create tension. To support students in answering Activity 5b and 5c, move them on to thinking about the impact of the symbolism: what mood or atmosphere is created by the juxtaposition of the two symbols?

⚙ Activity 6 Building your knowledge
Define the success criteria for this task with students before they attempt it, considering that students should use evidence from the text and the level of detail required in their analysis. Alternatively make Activity 6a an 'I do' and model the answer for students, 6b 'we do' and take input from the class, before 6c is independently completed as 'you do'.

⚙ Stretch yourself
Encourage students to consider their general knowledge of *Frankenstein*, which may be more than they realise – for example, the appearance of Frankenstein's monster masks at Halloween, or his appearance in *Hotel Transylvania* films.

Activity 7 Putting it all together
Direct students to the Kerboodle resource *Reading support* to help them with this activity, and their own notes or the teaching text to ensure their understanding of each convention as they identify it in the text. Students could build on their knowledge from Activity 6 to co-create success criteria and self- or peer-assess their answers against the success criteria once completed.

Additional activities
Explore film versions of both texts, showing the scenes in the films that are described in the extracts and ask students if they match their expectations. This can lead to discussion around the power of different interpretations.

Provide students with a stimulus picture or piece of music/soundscape and ask them to create their own gothic description applying the conventions they have learned about in this unit. Students could self-/peer-assess against a check-list of conventions. To develop this further, students could redraft their writing, this time focusing on developing a consistent atmosphere of mystery and fear, making careful vocabulary and language choices. Follow with a second round of self-/peer-assessment.

Unit focus

Objectives

Students will:

- learn how writers create sinister settings
- explore the use of language and structural techniques to build fear and tension
- write the opening of a story describing a sinister setting.

Unit texts

- 🔊 *Fog Island* Mariette Lindstein
- 🄚 *The Haunting of Hill House* Shirley Jackson **WS**

Assessment

🄚 2.2 Mini-checkpoint quiz

Key terms

- **juxtapose** to put words, ideas or images together to show a contrast or relationship between them
- **metaphor** a comparison that says one thing is something else, e.g. *Amy was a rock*
- **noun phrase** a noun plus information before and/or after the noun
- **simile** a comparison of one thing to another, using 'as' or 'like', e.g. *He swam like a fish*
- **suspense** a feeling of anxious uncertainty while waiting for something to happen or become known
- **tone** the writer's feeling or attitude expressed towards their subject

Introduction to the unit

Unit 2.2 *How can a setting create fear?* focuses on how writers create sinister settings, developing a deeper understanding of the writer's craft in creating suspense and tension. Students will read and explore the language choices within an extract from *Fog Island* by Mariette Lindstein. They will build on prior knowledge of gothic conventions to identify and analyse more sophisticated techniques such as juxtaposition, contrast and foreshadowing. Students can draw on their own experience of anticipation when watching dramas or reading, to understand with more clarity how techniques support the author's intentions. Finally, supported by a planning scaffold, students will draw on their prior knowledge and skills of structuring and description, and will apply their new knowledge of techniques in their own writing.

Activities

⚙ Starter activity

Discuss how the texts in Unit 2.1 made students feel, and their learning so far about how atmosphere is created. Ask: *Is the weather a useful way of creating atmosphere in a text? Why? Is personification a useful technique in gothic writing? Why?* Make links to gothic conventions such as the supernatural and isolated settings, etc. Bring the conversation back to how all these techniques make them feel. Do they enjoy having their feelings provoked in this way?

⚙ Activity 1

Activity 1a could encompass a huge array of fears, and the conversation will need to be conducted sensitively; try and focus on abstract fears rather than personal fears. Explore the differences between irrational fear (e.g. phobia of the number 13) and rational fear (e.g. skydiving) and knowing the difference between the two. Draw on gothic conventions in Activity 1b and explore how writers deliberately play on common fears to create suspense, resulting in excitement for some people while acknowledging that not everyone enjoys this type of entertainment.

Kerboodle

The following activities can be replaced by the text and activities on 2.2 *The Haunting of Hill House* worksheet.

Activity 2

Use this activity to secure students' understanding of the text; ask supplementary questions if necessary. Ask: *What are your initial feelings about the atmosphere and setting? Do you feel afraid, or perhaps curious?*

Activity 3 Boosting your vocabulary

Ask students to identify the verbs that describe the fog and rank them from least threatening to most threatening, highlighting increasing threat and tension in the text.

⚙ Activity 4 Building your knowledge

For further challenge, include techniques such as personification, pathetic fallacy or semantic fields; the different noises people make in reaction to the fog is a good example. For students who need support, model annotation, verbalising the thought process while taking input from students.

Activity 5 Building your knowledge

Use mini whiteboards so students can experiment with different examples. To scaffold the activity, provide a range of settings, moods and weather for students to mix and match in their sentences. As a class, discuss responses and demonstrate how contrasting descriptions change the tone and atmosphere in a text.

⚙ Activity 6 Building your knowledge

Elicit ideas about the forest environment that could hint at forthcoming problems, e.g. dappled light, low branches, leaves and twigs underfoot or bird calls, and prompt students to consider associated sounds, sights, smells, noises, textures. Explain that foreshadowing is a structural writing technique that students can transfer to their own future writing.

Activity 7 Building your knowledge

Decide in advance whether to deliver this activity as a class discussion or a written task. If the former, ask students to contribute a list of language and structural techniques and order them from most to

least impactful. Encourage students to 'think like a writer' and consider the author's intentions and deliberate choices by presenting alternatives. For example, what if the simile came later or the writer didn't contrast the weather between the day and night?

Activity 8 Putting it all together

Encourage students to refer back to their work from earlier in this unit to help them generate ideas and language devices. Mind-map ideas for Steps 1 and 2 as a class to consolidate new learning and address any misconceptions. If students need support with structure, suggest that they build on the approach of Activity 5, mirroring the wording of the extract but using their own different setting, a specific type of weather and versioning the use of personification, pathetic fallacy, vocabulary choices, etc. Remind them to 'show not tell' as they build foreshadowing into their plan. Encourage peer-assessment and redrafting.

Stretch yourself

Ask students to use different coloured highlighters to identify their use of figurative language, vocabulary choices and variety of sentence length and punctuation for impact. Then ask students to choose three examples from their writing and present an alternative version, using different language, sentence lengths or punctuation. Students should consider how this alters the atmosphere and mood of their writing.

Additional activities

Students could consolidate their learning from Units 2.1 and 2.2 by writing a 'how to' guide for creating sinister settings and characters.

As a challenge, they could have an additional focus in their writing on consistent use of ambitious vocabulary to create a specific tone or to develop and maintain a unique narrative voice. For example, students could identify 3–5 words in their work they want to improve and use a thesaurus to help them make vocabulary edits. A peer could suggest an adjective to describe the tone and identify any words that seem incongruous for the writer to reconsider and improve.

Unit focus

Objectives
Students will:
- learn how writers subvert and adapt genres over time
- explore the use of gothic conventions in contemporary stories
- comment on how a writer subverts gothic conventions to create fear and tension.

Unit texts
- 🔊 *Twilight* Stephenie Meyer
- 🔊 *A Monster Calls* Patrick Ness
- Ⓚ *Good Boy* Mal Peet **WS**

Assessment
- Ⓚ 2.3 Mini-checkpoint quiz

Key terms
- **antonym** a word that has the opposite meaning of a particular word
- **figurative language** words or phrases with a meaning that is different from the literal meaning
- **personification** showing something non-human as having human characteristics
- **prefix** a word or group of letters placed in front of another word to add to or change its meaning
- **subvert** to change an established way something is done

Introduction to the unit

Unit 2.3 *How do writers subvert a genre?* challenges students to apply their knowledge of gothic conventions to two extracts taken from contemporary gothic fiction: *Twilight* by Stephenie Meyer and *A Monster Calls* by Patrick Ness. Make cross-curricular links to Geography and History when considering towns and cities as impactful settings and explore the connotations of each. In this unit, the activities lead students to recall their knowledge of traditional gothic conventions from Unit 2.1 to identify how these are subverted in *Twilight*. The challenging concept 'subvert' may need contextualising, e.g. by linking it to popular culture that students may recognise, such as Disney's *Frozen*.

Students identify subverted conventions and consider their impact, in addition to identifying language and structural techniques used to impact the reader. Students will apply this sequential approach for independent analysis of an extract from *A Monster Calls* by Patrick Ness, during which they will identify gothic conventions and consider how and why the writer uses, adapts and subverts gothic conventions.

Activities

⚙ Starter activity
Recall prior knowledge by asking students to define the terms 'genre', 'convention' and 'gothic'. Explore the word 'subvert' as a class, using a Frayer model to ensure students have a deep understanding of the word and its use in different contexts. To help students attune to the concept of subverting conventions, discuss some familiar genres such as documentaries, reality TV and fairy tales, and consider examples of films, TV programmes and books that subvert their conventions, e.g. the film *Shrek*.

⚙ Activity 1

Highlight the process of returning to prior learning before embarking on a new activity, so as to build on a foundation of knowledge. Enthuse students by exploring how genres are subverted or intertwined in TV shows such as *Stranger Things* by playing scenes that show a mix of genre conventions.

Ⓚ Kerboodle

The following activities can be replaced by the text and activities on 2.3 *Good Boy* worksheet.

Activity 2 Boosting your vocabulary

To extend this activity, ask students to identify words Meyer uses in the extract to describe Phoenix and consider how a sense of contrast between the two places creates a feeling of foreboding.

⚙ Activity 3 Building your knowledge

Model and verbalise the thought process of analysing connotations of 'escaped'. It might be helpful to do some vocabulary work around the word 'omnipresent', considering the prefix 'omni'. Students may also be able to make links to prior knowledge from Unit 1, considering the work on 'light' and 'dark' and how this can be applied to the concept of 'shade' in this extract.

⚙ Activity 4 Building your knowledge

Model annotating the text to highlight and label the gothic features. If students struggle to identify the subverted conventions, highlight examples and demonstrate making the link with the traditional convention. Then ask students to consider how each one has been subverted. Involve students in considering the impact of each convention on the reader. Ask how students feel about the place or how they feel for the character who is going to live there, as a result of the convention used.

⚙ Activity 5 Building your knowledge

Students could work in pairs and 'coach' each other through this activity. For example: student A could complete Activity 5a and student B could

complete 5b. Rather than revealing and comparing answers, students support one another to complete the question they have not yet attempted by giving encouragement and even offering sentence starters to consolidate their own understanding of the strategies they have used.

Activity 6 Building your knowledge

Begin this activity by asking students: *Could you predict that vampires and the supernatural would be part of this story? How?* Discuss and share ideas.

⚙ Activity 7 Putting it all together

Point out to students that in the preceding tasks, they have already completed all the steps required for Activity 7, and they will now apply this knowledge independently.

Before students begin, ask them to consider their motivation for learning, and to anticipate any challenges they think they may face in this activity. Students could share these so, as a class, they can draw up strategies to help with any aspects they find tricky.

To approach the task, encourage students to look back at their own notes from the previous activities. To encourage independent learning, highlight the 'three before me' rule (if they get stuck, first ask themselves, then look in their book, then ask a peer). After the activity students could reflect on their experience and consider which strategies worked best for them.

Additional activities

Pose this question to students: *This chapter is called 'Terror and wonder'. To what extent do you think the authors of the extracts create either terror or wonder in their texts?* If students do not think terror or wonder are created by either text, what would they advise the authors to do to achieve these qualities?

Gothic is often a popular genre, so students could research contemporary gothic fiction aimed at young adults and create a reading list of books they would like to read, or visit the school/local library and find out what gothic fiction a librarian would suggest.

Unit focus

Objectives

Students will:

- learn how dramatists use language to control the reaction of their audience
- explore how figurative language, including imagery, can create fear and tension
- write and present a dramatic speech for a ghostly character.

Unit texts

- ◁》 *Hamlet* William Shakespeare
- Ⓚ *Richard III* William Shakespeare **WS**

Assessment

Ⓚ 2.4 Mini-checkpoint quiz; Chapter 2 Checkpoint 1 reading assessment; Chapter 2 Checkpoint 1 writing assessment

Key terms

- **connotation** an idea or feeling linked to a word, as well as its main meaning
- **emotive language** word choices that create a strong emotional reaction in the audience or reader
- **extended metaphor** a long metaphor which builds up an image in detail over many lines
- **gesture** using your hands to indicate meaning, e.g. to help emphasise certain points
- **imagery** language that creates pictures in the reader's mind
- **imperative** a sentence that gives an order, command or instruction
- **pace** the speed at which someone speaks or moves or something happens
- **repetition** using the same word or phrase more than once
- **rhetorical device** a language feature that has a persuasive or impressive effect on listeners and readers

Introduction to the unit

Unit 2.4 *How is figurative language used to create fear?* explores the presentation of ghosts in Shakespeare's play *Hamlet*. Explore key terms before reading the extract to ensure accessibility of the activities that follow. Ask students to consider why the idea of a ghost is such a significant one in literature, both as a literal feature and as a symbol. Alternatively, activate students' prior knowledge about drama texts and their conventions to ensure understanding before they read the extract.

Students will analyse Shakespeare's presentation of the ghost of Hamlet's father, looking at the use of figurative language and imagery to incite terror in the audience. Spend some time exploring the concept of symbols and how they can be used in literature and film. This unit focuses on the author's intentions; support students with some sentence starters that place the author at the centre of their analysis, e.g: *adverb, author's name, verb*: 'Notably Shakespeare creates…'.

Activities

Starter activity

Introduce the term 'imagery' and discuss what techniques are used to create imagery. Students could experiment out loud with different verbal descriptions of how they imagine a ghost might look, and compare this with their classmates' descriptions. Whose description was most effective in creating a picture in the reader's mind?

⚙ Activity 1

For Activity 1a, students should draw on prior knowledge of ghost stories in books, film and TV to think about reader/audience reactions. Encourage them to think about what gothic conventions they can identify in these stories and films. For 1b, activate prior learning about language features by asking them to explain what a simile or metaphor is before beginning the task.

Kerboodle

The following activities can be replaced by the text and activities on 2.4 *Richard III* worksheet.

⚙ Activity 2

Students should be encouraged to utilise their notes from previous units in Chapter 2 to answer this question. Extend this further by asking students why they think Shakespeare included a ghost in the play. Direct students to re-read What's the big idea? on page 82 of the Student Book which explains some of the possible functions of ghostly characters. From this, students can make their own interpretations of the intended function for the ghost in *Hamlet*.

Activity 3 Boosting your vocabulary

For Activity 3b provide a variety of sentence starters such as: *It was purged because… It was purged but… It was purged so…* to give students opportunity to show good understanding of the word. For 3c, discussing the connotations of the given words will give deeper meaning to word choice and the impact it has; e.g. 'justice' suggests law and order, and 'vengeance' suggests crime and violence.

⚙ Activity 4 Building your knowledge

Before starting this activity, re-affirm student understanding of the difference between simile and metaphor. Extended metaphor may be a new concept to many students; if so, they will need further examples from beyond the text to secure their understanding. To build students' confidence in undertaking detailed language analysis, create a model answer to Activity 4a, involving them in the process. Annotate the model to help students co-create success criteria for the subsequent activity parts. Inference and connotations of words will be important considerations; students should analyse the effects of these and what the reader's reactions might be. Generate a list of synonyms to which students can refer to support their analysis of reader reactions.

Activity 5 Building your knowledge

First, give students the opportunity to explore the concept of symbols in more depth. Display a number of common symbols such as a tree, a clock, a snake or a map and ask students to consider the connotations of each one. They could annotate the

pictures with their ideas in groups, and feed back to the class. Explain why symbols are used by writers and consequently the importance of inference when reading a literary text. If we believe literally that a snake killed Hamlet's father, then the current king he references would be a snake. Students need to understand that it is the connotations of the symbol that show what the writer is trying to say.

⚙ Activity 6 Building your knowledge

Remind students about rhetorical devices by directing them back to their notes from Chapter 1. To extend this activity, ask students to consider what purpose and function the character of the ghost serves – an interesting differentiation to acknowledge is the purpose of rhetorical devices in fictional texts as opposed to non-fiction.

Stretch yourself

Students could be further challenged to think of any examples that subvert the stereotypical view of snakes, for example Viper in *Kung Fu Panda*.

Activity 7 Building your knowledge

This activity gives students a chance to explore Shakespeare in the form in which it was meant to be seen. Ask students to act out the scene using different dramatic techniques to bring the character of the ghost to life. Confident students could act for the class and be peer-assessed on their use of dramatic techniques such as gesture and tone.

⚙ Activity 8 Putting it all together

This synoptic activity asks students to apply the skills and knowledge of this unit to their own writing. If stuck, students can refer back to the extract from *Hamlet* and find an example that they can adapt to fit their own work. More confident students can include examples of subverted gothic conventions.

Additional activities

Activity 8 provides another opportunity for students to perform their speech to a group of peers, and assess the performance against agreed success criteria.

To extend students' understanding of symbolism, set a task to research common literary symbols and create a mind map exploring their connotations.

Unit focus

Objectives

Students will:

- learn how a guide can combine instructions and advice
- explore how the structure and language features of a guide help to fulfil its purpose
- write a guide of their own, including instructions and advice.

Unit texts

- 🔊 'An astronomer's guide to stargazing with the naked eye' Mary McIntyre
- Ⓚ 'How to Set Up Your Smart Home' John R. Delaney and Whitson Gordon **WS**

Assessment

Ⓚ 2.5 Mini-checkpoint quiz

Key terms

- **ambiguity** having more than one meaning
- **colloquial language** informal words or phrases that are suitable for ordinary conversation, rather than formal speech or writing
- **homophone** a word that sounds the same as another, but is spelled differently and means something different
- **modal verb** a verb that works with another verb to show that something needs to happen or might possibly happen, e.g. *must, shall, will, should, would, can, could, may* and *might*
- **possessive determiner** a word that comes before a noun to show whose it is, e.g. *my, your, her*
- **second person** addressing the reader directly, using the pronoun 'you'

Introduction to the unit

Unit 2.5 *How do writers guide their readers?* introduces students to new text types – writing to advise and writing to instruct – and the form and purpose of these will be key to discussion and learning. Students will consider the differences between the text types and how they can be combined, building their understanding of the different techniques used to achieve each purpose, before applying this to their own writing. This unit presents a valuable opportunity to expand students' vocabulary and refresh their knowledge of grammar and sentence types, looking specifically at modal verbs, imperatives and determiners.

To help students to develop as independent learners, encourage them to self-assess throughout the unit, so that they are explicitly aware of the skills they are working on and can monitor and take responsibility for their own progress.

Activities

Starter activity

This chapter is called 'Terror and wonder'. Ask students what their immediate impressions of terror and wonder were before embarking on this chapter. Present students with a range of topics such as space, aliens, robots, vampires, ghosts, etc. and ask them to rank them on a continuum from terror to wonder. This could lead to a discussion around why stargazing and astronomy can incite both terror and wonder.

⚙ Activity 1

Build students' confidence by discussing as a class where they see instructional texts in their everyday lives, such as food packaging and new phones. Draw out the key features of instructional text that they are aware of, such as numbered steps and imperative verbs. Advice texts will be more challenging so present students with visual prompts such as an online 'agony aunt' advice page or a medical advice leaflet.

Kerboodle

The following activities can be replaced by the text and activities on 2.5 'How to Set Up Your Smart Home' worksheet.

Activity 2 Boosting your vocabulary

To deepen understanding of the word 'mesmerise', ask students to consider how well the word links to the chapter title 'Terror and wonder'. Ask: *Is it a good thing or a bad thing to be mesmerised?*

Introducing Activity 2c is a pertinent time to address other common homophones that students may confuse, for example: to/too; their/they're/there; weather/whether.

Activity 3 Building your knowledge

Encourage students to explain how they located the three main instructions. Highlight the skills of skimming and scanning. Ensure all students understand the terms 'imperatives', 'pronouns' and 'determiners' before they attempt this task. After they have completed Activity 3c, provide students with a chance to review and revise their work by asking them to annotate their own writing, as in 3a.

⚙ Activity 4 Building your knowledge

Begin by refreshing students' understanding of modal verbs and adverbs. Discuss the change of tone in a text when modal verbs rather than imperative verbs are used, and how this reflects the purpose of the text. For Activity 4d students should refer back to their notes and ideas from Activity 1, as well as note down the features identified in the teaching text on pages 91–92. To extend critical thinking, ask students when it is appropriate to include advice in an instructional text and when it isn't. Present different scenarios for students to identify the most appropriate text type – to instruct, advise or both, e.g.: how to build a piece of furniture; staying safe in the sun; how to make and decorate a cake.

⚙ Activity 5 Building your knowledge

To begin, students could co-create success criteria for this activity using their answer to Activity 4d as a guide. For less confident students, provide sentence starters and a selection of modal verbs they could

use alongside the examples provided in the fact file. More confident students could research the areas in the fact file and add in new facts about the areas, or use vocabulary to showcase and portray features of the areas in an exciting and appealing way.

⚙ Activity 6 Putting it all together

Students could complete the Kerboodle resources *Plan, monitor, evaluate* or *Preparing for writing* alongside this activity to support their planning and metacognitive thinking.

Lead a discussion for Step 1 to share ideas for the topic of their guide. Model verbalising the thinking behind ideas that give scope for instruction and those that would prompt more limited responses. Offer students a choice of audiences to select one that suits the selected topic. Model examples of vocabulary that would and would not support the tone for an instructional advisory text, e.g. sentences that are too demanding or patronising in tone. Model identifying, removing or changing unsuitable vocabulary. More confident students could complete Step 1 entirely independently and then present to a peer and justify their choices, using peer coaching questions such as: *Who is your audience? Why? What tone are you aiming to create? How will you do this?*

Draw attention to the checklists in Step 2 and ask students to highlight and label the features for writing to instruct and advise in their own work.

Additional activities

To extend students' understanding of tone in an advice text, ask students to create a text on a topic of their choice with a sympathetic, non-judgemental tone.

Explore example advice texts where there is a strong author voice and viewpoint: how does this impact on the reliability of the text? Do students think the reader's motivation to follow the advice is stronger or weaker?

Unit focus

Objectives
Students will:
- learn about explanation texts and their conventions
- explore the effects of structure and language features in an explanation text
- comment on how a writer uses the features of an explanation text in an article.

Unit texts
- ⊲») 'The Environmental Benefits of Driverless Cars' Ashleigh Rose-Harman
- Ⓚ 'Five ways AI is saving wildlife' Graeme Green **WS**

Assessment
Ⓚ 2.6 Mini-checkpoint quiz

Key terms
- **clause** a part of a sentence with its own verb
- **multi-clause sentence** a sentence with more than one clause, each with its own main verb, e.g. *The judge frowned and lifted her hammer.*

Introduction to the unit

Unit 2.6 *How do writers provide explanation?* continues to explore non-fiction texts through the topic of technology. Students will read and explore an explanation text, looking in detail at structural and language features. There is a keen focus on the impact of vocabulary on the reader, which supports students to develop a deeper understanding of how specific word choices can change how a text is received. By the end of the unit students will consolidate the knowledge and skills they have developed throughout the unit with an extended analytical response to the text. Make students aware of the transferability of the skills they have already utilised in Units 2.1–2.5 and in Chapter 1, and link this to the bigger picture of their future learning at KS4.

Activities

⚙ Starter activity
Facilitate a class discussion around environmental issues that could be solved by technology and students' own hopes for the future of technology and the environment. Students should recall knowledge from Unit 2.5 on the conventions of instructional and advice texts and make predictions on the similarities and differences between these texts and explanation texts.

⚙ Activity 1
Draw attention to what types of words students use to describe the images and discuss their connotations to explore deeper meanings and feelings about AI. For Activity 1b, debate the positives and negatives of artificial intelligence, perhaps showing examples of film trailers that exemplify this (e.g. *Wall-E, 2001: A Space Odyssey, Avengers: Age of Ultron*) to stimulate discussion.

⚙ Activity 2

Ask students what it means to 'explain' something. Explore possible different author intentions for an explanation text, e.g. they could be explaining to expose, to criticise, to persuade or to advocate. Discuss how this might impact the types of techniques or conventions authors would use or the tone they might create. Alternatively, work on the Starter activity in more depth by asking students to list features of texts that instruct or advise and noting these on the board. Work through the list of features and ask students to give a show of hands on whether they think each feature would be useful in a text that aims to explain.

🄺 Kerboodle

The following activities can be replaced by the text and activities on 2.6 'Five ways AI is saving wildlife' worksheet.

Activity 3 Boosting your vocabulary

Scaffold the activity by asking students to look at the four highlighted words in the source text: 'implications', 'manually', 'monitor', 'adhered'. Ask: *How do these relate to the purpose of the text? Would you expect to see such words in an explanation text about technology? Why/why not?* Extend the activity by asking students to identify other words that support the author's purpose, e.g. 'indirectly', 'contributing'. Explore how these create an element of evaluation in the text. Alternatively, students could identify the tier 3 vocabulary (e.g. 'autonomous', 'infra-red radars', 'motion sensors', 'GPS', 'complex algorithms') and explore how this contributes to tone and purpose.

Activity 4 Building your knowledge

Students may find it helpful to work in pairs or small groups to identify the structural features and their functions. For 4c, model a strategy for developing a successful summary, e.g. skimming the text for subheadings, to give students an example to facilitate their answers.

⚙ Activity 5 Building your knowledge

For Activity 5b, generate a word bank to support students with analysis of impact on the reader. This could include active verbs such as 'provokes' or 'highlights' and words to support identifying the effect such as 'question', 'realise', etc. Split the class into small groups and ask each to focus on a particular technique. Encourage students to share and discuss their answers.

Stretch yourself

Students could analyse how the tier 3 vocabulary affects the impact on the reader. To what extent would they trust the text without it? Encourage students to consider the implications of this task for their own writing: when is tier 3 vocabulary important in their other curriculum subjects and why?

⚙ Activity 6 Putting it all together

Encourage students to reflect on their learning so far and to look back at their completed work (particularly Activities 4 and 5). Draw out which knowledge and skills they can use in each section of their response. Ask them to identify any concerns about applying their knowledge to this final activity. This is a good time to address any misconceptions and for students to plan their response independently, seeking support as needed. Ask students to identify key features of the model answer to create a 'checklist for success'. After completing the task, students could self- or peer-assess against these criteria and generate a 'next steps' target for themselves using the relevant Kerboodle resources.

Additional activities

Ask students to rewrite the article as an opinion piece with a strong point of view and persuasive techniques to encourage the reader to adopt their view on driverless cars.

Unit focus

Objectives

Students will:

- learn how to structure a comparison of two texts
- explore how a writer's choice of language and register is shaped by purpose, audience and context
- compare two texts written on a similar topic.

Unit texts

- 🔊 'Meet the one-eyed robot – it's fantastic' Nicholas Lloyd
- 🔊 'Helping companies deploy AI models more responsibly' Zach Winn
- 🅚 'You'll Be Able To Carry Phone In Pocket In Future' **WS**
- 🅚 'Best smartphone 2023' Chris Rowlands **WS**

Assessment

🅚 2.7 Mini-checkpoint quiz

Key term

- **register** the manner of speaking or writing, which can range between formal and informal

Introduction to the unit

Unit 2.7 *How do we compare texts?* looks in more detail at the highly topical subject of artificial intelligence and robots. Share students' experiences, hopes and, potentially, fears for the future of AI and robots. The unit covers a broad range of skills and knowledge, and it will be helpful to revisit key terms before beginning the unit, e.g. 'register', 'topic', 'context', 'audience' and 'purpose'.

This skills-focused unit draws on students' prior experience and skills to consolidate and extend their knowledge of the writer's craft. Students will work with two texts separately, then identify similarities between them, e.g. topic, audience, purpose and register. This will help them to build up strategies for the final activity of writing a long-form comparison of the texts.

Activities

⚙ Starter activity

Prompt discussions around considerations authors might have to make, including word choice, register, text structure and tone. Ask: *How do we identify a text's audience and purpose? Why is it important to know the intended audience and purpose of a text? How does contextual information impact our understanding of a text?* This will help students to make more accurate predictions and link their ideas about a text to an author's intentions in their analysis.

⚙ Activity 1

To extend Activity 1a, more confident students could list comparative connectives and consider the impact of each one. Collect anonymised student responses to Activity 1b on sticky notes and use them to inform teaching and provide checkpoints to review students' confidence throughout the unit.

🅚 Kerboodle

The following activities can be replaced by the text and activities on 2.7 The future of mobile phones worksheet.

Activities 2 and 3

These activities check comprehension of the texts and inferred meanings, and analyse the authors' word choices. Ask students to identify the skills each question addresses so they think explicitly about how to approach their answers. To scaffold these activities, assign groups to each part of Activity 2 and discuss answers as a class, before students tackle Activity 3 independently.

Stretch yourself

Use the statements to stimulate group or whole-class debate. Invite opinions before encouraging students to support their ideas with textual evidence. More confident students could contribute a counter-argument to their own viewpoint.

Activity 4 Boosting your vocabulary

For part a, explore how the prefix 'in' means 'in', 'no' or 'not'. Ask students to explore this in the context of 'incorporates'. Consider words where this prefix has different meanings, e.g. 'independent', 'insufficient', 'insubordinate'. For part c, explain that 'audit' comes from the root word *audire* meaning 'to hear'. Ask how this links to 'audit' in this context. Explore other words with the same root. For deeper thinking, students could consider: *Can a robot act with integrity?*

⚙ Activity 5 Building your knowledge

Activities 5–10 cover the steps needed to build up to an analytical comparison of the texts. Note the steps on the board to draw attention to the strategies students need to employ; this could form success criteria for the final activity. Model scanning and annotating Text A to support students with retrieving information for Activity 5b, then ask them to look at Text B independently.

⚙ Activity 6 Building your knowledge

Students should engage their hinterland knowledge of text context. They can use the information above each extract but must also use their wider knowledge about technology in each time period to consider why the authors' viewpoints may differ.

Activity 7 Building your knowledge

Challenge students to link two purposes to specific language and structural techniques that support them. Ask why identifying the purpose and audience of a text is important in understanding the author's choices.

Activity 8 Building your knowledge

Encourage students to be specific in their audience classification, and to draw out specific words or references to audience in the texts that help them to determine who the audience is, e.g. Text A, a newspaper article, is likely to be aimed at people interested in current affairs, whereas Text B, from the technology website MIT News, is probably aimed at people interested specifically in technology.

Activity 9 Building your knowledge

Ask students to re-read page 98 of the Student Book independently, then share the language features mentioned. This will scaffold their second reading of the texts to identify the techniques used. In pairs, students could consider the impact of the techniques they identify on tone and register, and feed back to the class. Alternatively, model annotating the texts and use questions to encourage students to think about the impact of the techniques on tone and register.

⚙ Activity 10 Building your knowledge

This activity presents an opportunity for broader metacognitive reflection: ask students how they can prepare to approach a written task, e.g. rhetorical technique or figurative language checklists, sentence starters, sentence types and structure plans.

⚙ Activity 11 Putting it all together

Remind students that their answers to Activities 5–10 contain all the information they need to answer this question. Ask why it is helpful to plan their answer as a comparison table. Less confident students may benefit from a modelled paragraph. After completing the activity students could reflect on which of the strategies from Activities 5–10 worked best for them and which they need further support with. Alternatively, refer to the Kerboodle resource *Reflection questions* to generate discussion of strategies used.

Additional activities

Students could create their own piece of opinion writing on the topic of ethical use of AI in education. They could make a compelling case about why AI should be used for homework or consider concerns about plagiarism and the associated lack of independent thought.

Unit focus

Objectives

Students will:

- learn how an autobiography can inform and entertain a reader
- explore the conventions of autobiographies, such as the use of chronological order, the past tense, facts, opinions and description
- write an extract from their own autobiography about something they have done.

Unit texts

- ◁» *My Remarkable Journey: A Memoir* Katherine Johnson
- 🅚 *Limitless: The Autobiography* Tim Peake **WS**

Assessment

🅚 2.8 Mini-checkpoint quiz; Chapter 2 Checkpoint 2 writing assessment; Chapter 2 Checkpoint 2 reading assessment

Key terms

- **autobiography** the story of a person's life, written by that person
- **biography** the story of a person's life, written by someone else
- **chronological order** the order in which things happened
- **first-person narrative** a story told by someone as if they were involved in the events themselves, using first-person pronouns, e.g. *I* and *we*
- **past tense** a verb form that shows actions or events that have already happened
- **recount** an account (written or spoken) of an event or experience
- **third person** a narrative voice that informs the reader of what is taking place, using the pronouns *he*, *she* or *they*

Introduction to the unit

Unit 2.8 *How do writers present themselves?* explores the autobiographical account of Katherine Johnson, one of the first Black women to work as a NASA scientist. The text draws on history and culture and reflects on current discourses surrounding women in the workplace, specifically on diversity in the STEM field. Help students understand the significance of this extract and Johnson's place in history. The themes of race and sexism are both touched upon in this extract. Draw attention to this and the ways in which students should discuss such topics respectfully.

Students will apply skills practised in previous units to a new genre type: autobiography. They will explore the autobiographical features present in Johnson's writing before completing their own piece of autobiographical writing. Encourage students to utilise skills practised in Units 1–4 for creative writing, as well as skills explored in Units 5–7 to consolidate their learning from across the chapter as a whole.

Activities

Starter activity

Engage students by exploring the idea of space travel. Display pictures of space and ask students to think of adjectives to describe them. Allow students to explore how and why space creates terror and wonder.

⚙ Activity 1

The role social media plays will be an engaging discussion point, as it brings people closer than ever to those they admire (especially celebrities). Explore the word 'autobiography', paying attention to the root words 'auto', 'bio' and 'graph'.

Kerboodle

The following activities can be replaced by the text and activities on 2.8 *Limitless: The Autobiography* worksheet.

Activity 2 Boosting your vocabulary

To encourage deeper thinking, ask students why, given the context of the text, Johnson needed to be assertive and therefore why 'collaboration' was essential for her.

Activity 3 Building your knowledge

Use this activity to identify areas for development in tenses by addressing common mistakes when writing in the past tense, e.g. inconsistent use of tense, mixing up simple past and continuous past. In part b, ensure students understand the term 'biography' and discuss the impact of first person versus third person; ask students why people might read a biography instead of an autobiography, addressing how this affects the form and purpose. Challenge more confident students to vary sentence openings so that not all sentences begin with 'I'.

Activity 4 Building your knowledge

Ask students to consider why a recount is usually written in chronological order, taking into account the audience and purpose of the text. To challenge students, consider the impact of using chronological order rather than non-linear structures.

Activity 5 Building your knowledge

Discuss the unique perspective an autobiography offers compared with a biography. Discuss the insight into feelings and opinions given firsthand, and also the reliability of the recount. Split the class into groups of three to complete the task: one group for facts, one for opinions and one for feelings. One student from each group could move to another group to 'retrieve and report back'.

⚙ Activity 6 Building your knowledge

Ask students to think about the connotations of the words and phrases they identify in part a. Students could 'explode' the simile in part b – picking out words that have the greatest impact on the reader and exploring the connotations. For part c give students a focus for their sentence, e.g. waiting at the start of a race.

Stretch yourself

To break this task down, ask students to identify the tier 3 specialist vocabulary and explore its impact. Discuss Johnson's use of this language given the context in which she worked. Students could then identify the colloquial language and consider how the mix of the 'professional' and the 'personal' contributes to the reader's opinion of the writer.

Activity 7 Putting it all together

Support students by scaffolding the process:

- mind-map possible memory ideas and select the strongest, most interesting idea
- break the event down into 3–5 key parts to form paragraphs
- build up ideas of what to include in each paragraph, considering the five senses and the checklist in the Student Book
- consider the intended effect on the reader's *feelings* about this event and the role of the writer in it. How will they create the right tone for their recount?

To extend, ask students to consider their use of colloquial language to present a more personal side of themselves.

Ask students to review their work against the listed key conventions in the activity box, highlighting and labelling the features in their writing and identifying areas where they need support.

Stretch yourself

Students could consider how and why they might use a different tone and register, perhaps to aim their writing at a younger audience, or one more interested in the topic of their writing. After completing their rewrite, students could reflect on the different choices they made, how they identified which words to change, and which version they prefer and why.

Additional activities

Students could write an argument or hold a class debate on the topic of equality. Ask: *Are women today given the same opportunities as men?* Remind students to respect one another's views. Give students an opportunity to research the topic so it can remain strictly factual.

3 Wild places and urban landscapes

 ## Chapter overview

Throughout this chapter, students will study texts that reflect writers' attitudes towards a variety of places, from the built environment of cities and suburbia, to rural wildscapes and the coast, as well as those liminal zones known as 'edgelands'. Students will explore the vitality of space as mediated through different voices and forms, including poetry, fiction and non-fiction; from 19th century texts to contemporary blogs. Students will develop a deeper understanding of how setting is integral to narrative and how places reflect a writer's attitudes and perspectives.

Each unit develops knowledge and skills learned in previous units. Core knowledge about narrative structure, the connection between language and identity, text as construct, the writer's voice, and the importance of context to both the production and reception of texts will be revisited in a number of units. Students continue to encounter a range of fiction and non-fiction genres and their knowledge of poetry will extend to a study of Romantic poets in Unit 3.3.

Furthermore, this chapter draws fascinating links between content covered earlier in the book. For example, Unit 6 looks at the notion of 'intertextuality', in particular the conventions of the ghost story, thus recalling Chapter 2's focus on terror and wonder; Unit 7 explores environmental concerns through the study of rhetoric, thus linking to power and influence in Chapter 1.

In addition, this chapter looks forward to Quest 3. Unit 3.8 addresses contemporary concerns about the environment which will be explored in more detail in Quest 3 Chapter 2 *Utopia and dystopia*. This chapter also helps students develop the knowledge and skills essential for future English studies at Key Stage 4 and beyond. Throughout, students will be given opportunities to evaluate and form opinions about texts which are rooted in critical analysis. Through this, they continue their own journey of discovery, building more expert networks of understanding that will, inevitably, help them to become more confident students of English.

  ## Texts

The texts in this chapter have been selected for their diversity, challenge and richness of language. There is an eclectic mix of genres: travel writing, Romantic poetry and eco-fiction sit alongside environmental activism, nature writing and contemporary Young Adult fiction. Many of the writers and texts will be new to students, thus extending their disciplinary knowledge. Exciting new voices such as Tahereh Mafi and Dr Mya-Rose Craig are joined by the canonical (William Wordsworth and J. B. Priestley) and the familiar (Bill Bryson); Romantic poetry is represented by Charlotte Smith while Sam Selvon's *The Lonely Londoners* offers an insight into the importance of language and identity. Consequently, the material is challenging and thought-provoking. Issues as varied as the impact of 9/11 upon young people; the generation gap caused by repeated failure to address environmental crises; the sense of alienation felt by arriving in a new place: all offer opportunities for rich and dynamic classroom discussion to which students can bring their own valuable experiences.

Key

k Kerboodle

◁)) Audio

Reading skill

Writing skill

Speaking and listening skill

WS Worksheet

3A Wild places and urban landscapes

Unit	Texts	Objectives
1 How are attitudes towards place conveyed?	• ◁» Letter from Charles Lamb to William Wordsworth, 1801 • ◁» *A Book of Silence* Sara Maitland • Ⓚ *English Journey* J. B. Priestley **WS** • Ⓚ *The Lost Continent* Bill Bryson **WS**	• Learn how writers reveal attitudes towards place • Explore what is meant by a writer's tone • Compare how two writers convey attitudes towards place
2 How are new places presented in literature?	• ◁» *The Lonely Londoners* Sam Selvon • Ⓚ *A Beginner's Guide to Acting English* Shappi Khorsandi **WS**	• Learn how writers use narrative voice to describe unfamiliar places • Consider how language choices and narrative voice create character and place • Write a short description of an unfamiliar place using a distinctive narrative voice
3 How do poets present the power of nature?	• ◁» 'Written near a port on a dark evening' Charlotte Smith • Ⓚ 'Composed upon Westminster Bridge, September 3, 1802' William Wordsworth **WS**	• Learn how a poet conveys the power of a natural landscape • Explore how poetic structure and imagery are used to create mood • Analyse a poem for what it reveals about the poet's attitude to nature
4 How is setting used to create tension?	• ◁» *An Emotion of Great Delight* Tahereh Mafi • Ⓚ *Anita and Me* Meera Syal **WS**	• Learn how writers use setting to create narrative tension • Explore how narrative perspective, foreshadowing and sensory description help to build tension • Write the opening of a story, using descriptions of the setting to build tension

Checkpoint Assessment: Chapter 3 Checkpoint 1 reading assessment; Chapter 3 Checkpoint 1 writing assessment

3B Wild places and urban landscapes

Unit	Texts	Objectives
5 How do writers make ordinary places interesting?	• ◁» *The Unofficial Countryside* Richard Mabey • Ⓚ 'A Walk on the Wild Side' Sarah Gardner **WS**	• Learn how writers actively influence the reader's attitude towards place • Explore how juxtaposition, descriptive detail and language choices build up a sense of place • Comment on how a writer influences your attitude towards a place
6 How are shifting landscapes presented?	• ◁» *The Easternmost House* Juliet Blaxland • Ⓚ *The Feast* Margaret Kennedy **WS**	• Learn how a writer uses shifting landscapes to create contrasting moods • Explore how writers borrow styles from other genres • Write about a place, creating contrasting moods
7 How can we write about environmental issues?	• ◁» 'Taking our future into our own hands' Dr Mya-Rose Craig • Ⓚ Severn Cullis-Suzuki's speech, 1992 **WS**	• Learn more about rhetorical skills • Explore how to structure and present an argument • Write and present your point of view about an environmental issue
8 How do writers describe future spaces?	• ◁» *Exodus* Julie Bertagna • Ⓚ *Memory of Water* Emmi Itäranta **WS**	• Learn about the subgenre of climate fiction • Understand what is meant by exposition in a narrative • Consider the ways in which a writer presents future worlds

Checkpoint Assessment: Chapter 3 Checkpoint 2 reading assessment; Chapter 3 Checkpoint 2 writing assessment

⭐ Background knowledge

This chapter introduces representations of, and attitudes towards, settings in literary and non-literary texts. Students will learn about mood, tone, atmosphere and how these are modulated by a writer's use of language. Students will develop their knowledge of text structures and forms, ranging from sonnets and speeches to non-fiction nature writing and contemporary literature.

Before delving into this chapter, teachers might ask students to consider their own experiences of familiar and unfamiliar places, including those they have experienced vicariously through film and literature. Students may be familiar with some literary constructions of place, e.g. William Blake's *London*, where setting is used to comment on political and social themes. Tom Becker's *Darkside* takes a different approach to how social division is mediated through urban space. Clive King's *Stig of the Dump* considers wasteland, while Darren Simpson's modern equivalent *Scavengers* uses an alternative perspective. Students may have watched films where setting is fundamental, e.g. Peter Jackson's *The Lord of the Rings* trilogy draws on Tolkien's oppositions of rural = idyllic versus city = danger.

Discussions can be had about how we respond to representations of urban and rural space. This will vary depending on the context of the school. Students' own experiences may contradict spatial stereotypes of rural idylls, cosy suburban life and 'gritty' images of the city. Explore whether students are aware of the social or political construction of space, e.g. green spaces that become a housing estate or a shopping centre. Mediate with care more sensitive topics in texts, e.g. separation from a homeland, with sensitivity towards students' cultural, social and economic backgrounds, and life experiences.

⬡ Cross-curricular links

This chapter has boundless connections to Geography. Unit 5 enables students to consider how urban development impacts on wildlife and how nature finds ways to flourish even in built-up areas. Contemporary ecological concerns are voiced by ornithologist Dr Mya-Rose Craig. Students can make links with History by thinking about the Industrial Revolution in Units 1 and 3, and develop awareness of political issues in Unit 7 where they consider environmental activism and their own social development. There is a strong visual element in this chapter: the photographs illuminate the textual concepts and offer opportunities to explore the power of the visual as a medium for communication, and so make links with Art as well as Film and Media Studies.

Finally, the vocabulary introduced in this chapter embeds cross-disciplinary knowledge and exposes how the changing landscapes impact our vocabulary today: new concepts such as 'edgelands' and language of natural and urban landscapes which introduces new tier 2 and tier 3 words, e.g. 'moorland', 'magpies', 'relics' and 'reedcutters'.

🌿 Representation and inclusion

This chapter includes texts from writers encompassing a variety of cultures, nationalities and ethnicities, enabling students to consider familiar places from alternative perspectives. Seeing historical events through the eyes of those affected is vital for developing empathy: in Unit 4, the extract from Tahereh Mafi's novel *An Emotion of Great Delight* allows students to see this impact, literally at ground level. They will also read about the post-colonial experiences of writers who have experienced migration or fled oppression.

It is important to consider the sensitivity of the material. For example, students with links to the Windrush generation will relate to the experiences in Sam Selvon's *The Lonely Londoners*; some students may have experienced the casual racism towards Tahereh Mafi's Muslim narrator. Furthermore, Mafi's narrator describes the environment by focusing on senses other than sight; this may provide both challenges and opportunities for some students.

🄚 Kerboodle texts

Several alternative routes are offered on Kerboodle, so students can follow the same learning objectives in each unit while focusing on text choices that best suit their ability profile or interests. The texts range across several centuries, reflecting both male and female perspectives, as well as different cultural views, including an excerpt from *A Beginner's Guide to Acting English* by Shappi Khorsandi; Meera Syal's *Anita and Me*; and Severn Cullis-Suzuki's speech at the 1992 Rio Earth Summit.

💬 Assessment

Mini-checkpoint quizzes, with automatic next steps built in, can be completed by students after each unit.

Spelling, punctuation and grammar mini-checkpoint quizzes can also be completed after every two units. These quizzes can be used to reinforce learning that students acquired in Year 7 or be used to support any spelling, punctuation and grammar lessons that are being undertaken in Year 8.

Checkpoint assessments are available to students after every fourth unit, after each part of the chapter. These assess students' knowledge, and skills are based on the core skills in the Quest assessment levels. Students can use the *Assessment wrapper* resource on Kerboodle while undertaking these assessments, which comprises a pre-assessment and post-assessment reflection exercise to help plan and review what they have learned.

✵ Further reading

The books and playscript below will complement the units in Chapter 3 and could be used in whole-class reading, as a class reader or in a drama session.

The Rollercoaster titles have online resource packs which will be useful when planning.

Rollercoaster *Scavengers* Darren Simpson

Rollercoaster *Where the World Ends* Geraldine McCaughrean

RSC Schools Shakespeare *A Midsummer Night's Dream* William Shakespeare

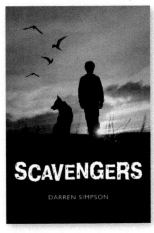

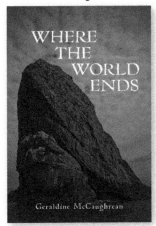

Chapter opener

✷ How to use the chapter opener

The chapter opener includes an introduction to the units with some questions to prompt students to think about the topic and to recall prior learning. The chapter opener will help prepare students in understanding the texts covered in the units. It can be used to initiate a discussion about what content students think might be covered in the chapter and to explore any background knowledge they have, or might need to have. It can also be used to help students review their understanding at the end of the chapter and discuss what they have learned.

Look at some examples of maps. Ask: *What information do they give us about a place? Where else might you find information about a place?* List these sources and decide how reliable each one might be.

Discuss the nuances of words such as 'place', 'location', 'space'. In what situations have students encountered these words? How many different ways can students use these words?

Discuss what is meant by 'setting'. Use examples from literature (e.g. the opening to *Bleak House* by Charles Dickens) to think about how a writer's tone can affect the reader's reaction to a place.

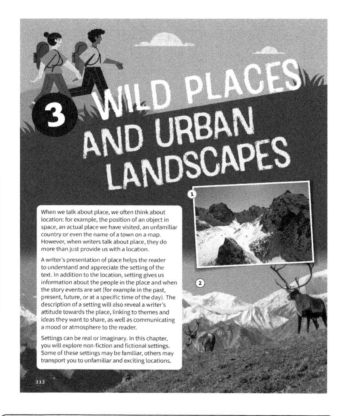

3 WILD PLACES AND URBAN LANDSCAPES

When we talk about place, we often think about location: for example, the position of an object in space, an actual place we have visited, an unfamiliar country or even the name of a town on a map. However, when writers talk about place, they do more than just provide us with a location.

A writer's presentation of place helps the reader to understand and appreciate the setting of the text. In addition to the location, setting gives us information about the people in the place and when the story events are set (for example in the past, present, future, or at a specific time of the day). The description of a setting will also reveal a writer's attitude towards the place, linking to themes and ideas they want to share, as well as communicating a mood or atmosphere to the reader.

Settings can be real or imaginary. In this chapter, you will explore non-fiction and fictional settings. Some of these settings may be familiar, others may transport you to unfamiliar and exciting locations.

112

Another way in might be to look at stills from different film genres: gothic horror, science fiction, fantasy, etc. Ask: *What is the iconography of space?* By this, we mean the motifs, common objects and architecture that are associated with a genre. How would students know they were looking at a still from a horror film, for example?

Provide students with a range of extracts describing a place. Combine fiction and non-fiction (e.g. extracts from travel brochures and guides, encyclopedia entries, travel writing). Ask students to place them on a continuum depending on whether they are fact or fiction. Explore the language used and how easy (or difficult) it is to discern fact from fiction.

Part a is a good opportunity to explore local context as well as for students to share experiences. Ask students to rate some local places such as the park, leisure facilities, shopping centres, school. Use selected criteria such as appearance, utilities and resources, proximity, etc.

Part b can include film, TV drama, games, comics and graphic novels. Students may refer to examples such as Hogwarts, Narnia, Mordor, etc. Ask students to think about why they are memorable. Is it the events that occurred there? The characters they associate with the place? The physical description? It might also be interesting to think about how their attitude to these places may have changed as they have got older.

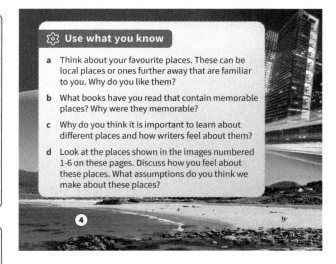

⚙ Use what you know

a   Think about your favourite places. These can be local places or ones further away that are familiar to you. Why do you like them?

b   What books have you read that contain memorable places? Why were they memorable?

c   Why do you think it is important to learn about different places and how writers feel about them?

d   Look at the places shown in the images numbered 1-6 on these pages. Discuss how you feel about these places. What assumptions do you think we make about these places?

④

Part c is probably one of the most important discussions to have in the context of this chapter. Ask students to think about how they would know about other places – whether real or imaginary – if they hadn't read about them or seen them on TV. Draw out big ideas such as empathy and compassion, broadening cultural capital, and being able to relate to the experience of different places.

Part d could be scaffolded by providing students with some vocabulary to use in their responses.

Discuss the concept of stereotypes and preconceptions and link this to the word 'assumptions'. Introduce words such as 'isolation', 'community', 'variety', 'excitement', 'tranquility', 'vulnerability', 'neighbourhood', 'pollution', 'expense', 'tourism', etc. Spark a debate about the pros and cons of each setting and about students' own preconceptions and misconceptions.

Key vocabulary

The vocabulary introduced in the chapter opener forms the basis for the subsequent topics in the Student Book. These specialist items of terminology are building blocks for students to become familiar with and to begin to use with confidence in response to texts.

Students will have met much of this vocabulary during KS1 and KS2. However, some students may struggle to visualise the more abstract concepts. Visual reminders on classroom wall displays may help, as well as providing definitions to reinforce the meanings.

Explore the chapter's key words through activities:

1   Students could explore some of these words using Frayer diagrams.

2   Find images to go with each word.

3   Use each word in a sentence.

4   Explore the etymology of some words, e.g. 'landscape'. What does this reveal about the word?

5   Which can be nouns, which are adjectives, which are verbs? How does changing the word class ('marginal' to 'marginalised', for example) alter the connotations?

Words you need to know

landscape, urban, rural, marginal, futuristic, environment, climate fiction, coast, nature, wasteland

⚙ How to use the learning overview

The learning overview provides students with a unit-by-unit breakdown of what to expect in the chapter. The aim of the learning overview is to:

- activate prior knowledge
- demonstrate the sequential learning that students will undertake so they can make connections between their learning from one unit to the next
- illustrate the bigger picture of what students will learn so they understand how each unit builds their knowledge and skills to succeed in the English curriculum, and so they can apply knowledge to the real world
- give students the opportunity to practise self-regulation in the face of new learning by considering motivation and how to approach potential challenges in the units ahead.

Each box within the learning overview asks students a question (Prepare) to help them activate their prior learning for that unit before explaining the 'what' and the 'how': what students can expect to learn in the unit (What I will learn) and the tasks they can expect to complete (How I will learn). Each chapter's unique learning overview provides prompts and mini-activities to encourage and engage students ahead of the primary work.

3.1 Prepare: Ask students to think about why they might visit a city or the countryside. Show them relevant images, or even explore tourist guides or travel brochures to give students an idea of what attracts people to these places.

3.3 Prepare: Read some examples of Romantic poetry, e.g. *Songs of Innocence* by William Blake, 'To Autumn' by John Keats or extracts from *Lyrical Ballads* by William Wordsworth and Samuel Taylor Coleridge. Discuss the mood of the poems and how these poets present the natural world.

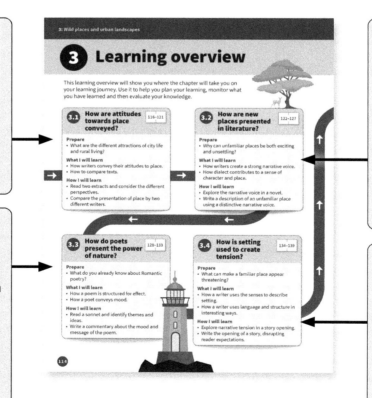

3.2 What I will learn: Discuss students' own dialects and accents or listen to some regional accents on websites such as YouTube, etc. Find out which parts of the country these dialects are spoken in to reinforce the links between dialect and place.

3.4 How I will learn: Show some appropriate tense scenes from films or TV and discuss how they create impact. Read dramatic extracts from famous novels and explore how the writers develop suspense.

3.5 What I will learn: Show images of wasteland, disused factories and derelict buildings. Discuss students' reactions to these places. Consider why some people might be fascinated with such places.

3.7 Prepare: Ask students to think about some of the persuasive devices they may have learned about in previous units. Listen to some famous speeches and think about how the speakers use tone and intonation to convey their message.

3.6 How I will learn: Ask students to consider how a place can provoke different moods, e.g. a beach can feel calm when empty, but overwhelming when crowded with tourists. Students could think about how the same place could therefore be used as the setting for either a ghost story or an adventure story.

3.8 Prepare: In preparation for understanding climate fiction as a subgenre of science fiction, students could discuss how the environment is under threat and what might be the consequences of inaction. They could then think about films and stories that deal with environmental and climate catastrophe, e.g. *Avatar*.

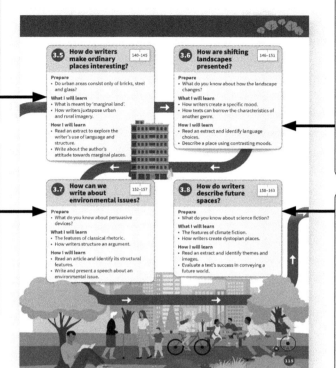

⚙ Metacognition

The activities in each chapter set out to make the implicit, explicit: to draw out what many students will already intuitively know but not necessarily be aware of knowing.

On Kerboodle, metacognitive resources are available to use alongside teaching and to support students throughout the chapter and while completing activities.

- *Pre-chapter reflection* supports students to engage with the content within the chapter opener and learning overview.
- *Post-chapter reflection* supports students at the end of chapters to reflect on and consolidate their learning.
- *Reading support* can be used alongside each source text so students can independently access an unseen text.
- *Preparing for writing* and *Preparing for reading* can be used to support students undertaking an extended reading and writing tasks, particularly for the Putting it all together activities.
- *Reflection questions* can be used at any point during a lesson to delve further into students' thinking and identify where they can implement skills strategically.
- *Plan, monitor, evaluate* helps students to constructively approach the Putting it all together activities.
- *Learning log* can be used by students to summarise their learning at the end of every unit. This can be referred to for revision throughout students' KS3 learning.
- *Assessment wrapper* can be used alongside longer summative assessments to assess students' confidence, planning and self-regulation.
- *Self-regulation* can be used at the start of a task, unit or chapter to assess students' confidence and motivation.

Unit focus

Objectives

Students will:

- learn how writers reveal attitudes towards place
- explore what is meant by a writer's tone
- compare how two writers convey attitudes towards place.

Unit texts

- 🔊 Letter from Charles Lamb to William Wordsworth, 1801
- 🔊 *A Book of Silence* Sara Maitland
- Ⓚ *English Journey* J. B. Priestley **WS**
- Ⓚ *The Lost Continent* Bill Bryson **WS**

Assessment

Ⓚ 3.1 Mini-checkpoint quiz

Key terms

- **figurative language** words or phrases with a meaning that is different from the literal meaning
- **narrator** a person who tells a story, especially in a book, play or film
- **root** the core of a word that has meaning. It may or may not be a complete word
- **setting** where the action takes place
- **tone** the writer's (or speaker's) feeling or attitude expressed towards their subject

Introduction to the unit

Unit 3.1 *How are attitudes towards place conveyed?* prompts students to reflect on attitudes towards rural and urban spaces. Students will analyse and compare a 19th century text and a 21st century text, focusing on how tone and perspective are achieved through the writers' use of language. Prior knowledge of Romantic poets is not needed in this unit, however it presents a fruitful opportunity to introduce or refresh students' knowledge of this interesting area of literature.

Activities

Starter activity

This unit introduces the concepts of tone and perspective. To think about tone, ask students to repeat some everyday phrases or lines from a class text in different tones of voice. Discuss how tone changes meaning. Challenge students to find texts in print or other media which offer different perspectives on the same places; they could keep a journal and collect texts that focus on place.

⚙ Activity 1

This could be set as a flipped learning task, with students bringing in powerful or exciting images they have found at home, ready for classroom discussion. Explore the word 'memorable' and draw out that it doesn't always have positive connotations.

Ⓚ Kerboodle

The following activities can be replaced by the text and activities on 3.1 Attitudes to place worksheet.

Activity 2

The images in Activity 2 provide a clear representation of the locations Lamb mentions in the source text, supporting students who are unfamiliar with either London or the Lake District. The vocabulary can be used to draw out the different connotations and applications of the words: e.g. 'dangerous' could describe either location – encourage students to articulate *why*.

⚙ Activity 3 Boosting your vocabulary

This activity focuses on both morphology (the study of the form of words) and etymology. Encourage students to draw on prior knowledge of etymology from Unit 1.1 *How do speakers use language to influence?* Explain that root words can be misleading; the exploration of *satis* requires students to think about how words evolve. Extend part b by looking at the word 'pantomime' which derives from the Greek word *pantomimos*, meaning 'imitator of all'. Link the idea of pantomimes, which involve audience participation, and the prefix 'pan', meaning 'all'. What other words use the prefix 'pan'?

Activity 4 Building your knowledge

For Activities 4a and 4b, ask students to note down the nouns in the text and categorise them as 'people', 'places', 'proper nouns', 'feelings', 'objects and things'. They could also look at nouns that work as metaphors ('pantomime', 'masquerade') and abstract nouns ('emotions'). To extend this task, students could look at how Lamb uses adjectives to *modify* the nouns, e.g. 'dead nature' creates a strong impression of how Lamb negatively views life in the country, as well as creating an oxymoron. For Activity 4c, it might be helpful to show images of a pantomime and a masquerade. For 4d students could match quotations to the words in Activity 2a.

Stretch yourself

This activity requires some scaffolding: provide brief background information on Wordsworth's love of nature to help students develop a counter-argument to Lamb's letter. Ask: *What do you think Lamb means when he says, 'All these emotions must be strange to you'?* Model opening sentences and follow the 'I do/ we do/you do' approach.

Activity 5 Building your knowledge

Maitland's text is rich with imagery and full of movement like Lamb's, only this time it focuses on nature. Draw attention to the moors of England which are the setting for some classic novels, e.g. Emily Brontë's *Wuthering Heights* and Arthur Conan Doyle's *The Hound of the Baskervilles*. In Activity 5a, explore the scope of Maitland's text and discuss the concept of lexical fields (words that connect to a particular topic, e.g. rain, snow and ice connect to the lexical field of weather). Students could use different colours to note down details relevant to the four features. Scaffold this activity by pre-selecting appropriate textual details along with their effects and asking students to match them. Activity 5c provides an opportunity to talk about paragraph construction. Use the example in the Student Book as a model, showing how it begins with a big idea as a topic sentence, and then drills down into the specifics by selecting appropriate textual detail and then analysing key words. Consider pairing students for peer review after the task, with one less confident and one more confident student working together to review and improve work where necessary.

Activity 6 Putting it all together

Students may need to do some preliminary work on the given vocabulary in Step 1. Finding synonyms is always useful, e.g. 'cheerful' might yield 'happy', 'jolly', 'contented' and 'untroubled'. In Step 2, support less confident students by pre-selecting a few quotations for each word and discussing with students which is the most precise one. The example in the table provides a scaffold for Step 3. For Step 4, remind students to look at similarities as well as differences when comparing texts. Co-create success criteria before students start writing, drawing out the need to identify relevant evidence from the text to exemplify both the details the writers focus on, and the language which contributes to the overall tone of each piece.

Additional activities

Students could work in pairs in role as Lamb and Maitland, each arguing that their location is more exciting than the other. These could be presented to the class, drawing on the debate skills learned in Unit 1.3 *What is a debate?*

Unit focus

Objectives

Students will:

- learn how writers use narrative voice to describe unfamiliar places
- consider how language choices and narrative voice create character and place
- write a short description of an unfamiliar place using a distinctive narrative voice.

Unit texts

- ◁» *The Lonely Londoners* Sam Selvon
- **ⓚ** *A Beginner's Guide to Acting English* Shappi Khorsandi **WS**

Assessment

ⓚ 3.2 Mini-checkpoint quiz

Key terms

- **clause** a part of a sentence with its own verb
- **colloquial language** informal words or phrases that are suitable for ordinary conversation, rather than formal speech or writing
- **complex sentence** a multiclause sentence with at least one subordinate clause, e.g. *He stopped because he was tired.*
- **context** the time, place and influences on a text from when it was written, and from when it is read, which shape our understanding of the text
- **dialect** a form of language linked to a specific region, e.g. Geordie in Newcastle upon Tyne
- **narrative voice** the perspective (viewpoint) from which a story is told, and the style in which it is told
- **present tense** a verb form that describes actions which are happening now
- **pronoun** a word used instead of a noun or noun phrase, e.g. *he, it, they*
- **pronunciation** the sound made when a word is spoken
- **repetition** using the same word or phrase more than once
- **rhetorical question** a question asked for dramatic effect and not intended to get an answer
- **Standard English** a widely recognised, formal version of English, not linked to any region, but used in schools, exams, official publications and in public announcements
- **synonym** a word or phrase that means the same, or almost the same, as another word or phrase

Introduction to the unit

Unit 3.2 *How are new places presented in literature?* explores how an author can create a sense of dislocation with a place in their writing. In contrast to Unit 3.1 where students learned how a writer's selection of familiar details contributed to understanding their perspective, in this unit, Sam Selvon depicts a Caribbean migrant's experience of an unfamiliar London. While Lamb and Maitland are at home in their settings in Unit 3.1, the narrator Galahad feels like an outsider.

This unit also introduces the notion of dialect and accent and asks students to consider the links between language and power. Before students read the text, some preliminary work on the colonialist background as context for attitudes towards accents and dialects might prove useful; a sensitive discussion will be needed as this will be close to some students' cultural experiences. The Did you know? and context sections provide information on Windrush and migration; however, teachers may wish to introduce some news accounts to contextualise this topic further.

Activities

Starter activity

Encourage students to find texts written using dialect, informal and non-standard forms, such as the poetry of Jon Agard and Grace Nichols. Explain the differences between dialect and Standard English, rejecting prejudices and preconceptions. Take care to explain the importance of context as well as the links between dialect/accent and environment.

 Activity 1

Lead this activity as a class discussion. To begin, display images of 'outsiders' in popular media such as Harry Potter arriving in Diagon Alley, or for a more challenging and political discussion, people disembarking from the Windrush. This encourages students to see through the eyes of someone else, and will encourage them to think of their own experiences of being in an unfamiliar place and their emotional response.

Ⓚ Kerboodle

The following activities can be replaced by the text and activities on 3.2 *A Beginner's Guide to Acting English* worksheet.

Activity 2 Boosting your vocabulary

Working with synonyms helps students to nuance their own writing – remind students of the work they did on synonyms in Unit 3.1 Activity 6.

Activity 3 Building your knowledge

This activity helps students to develop an understanding of language and context, and to make links between standard forms of a language with power, status and authority. All of the statements in part c are valid, so there is scope for interesting discussion here. Students could work in groups of three with each given one of the statements. It is then their task to provide reasons to convince other students that their reason is the most important.

Activity 4 Building your knowledge

This synoptic activity draws together the reading knowledge and skills acquired in this unit. Setting up discussion groups prior to this activity will encourage students to share ideas. A mix of less confident and more confident students will help all students engage with this discussion focus. The consensus circle strategy could be useful here: students could write their ideas on sticky notes, then discuss which ideas are most valid.

Activity 5 Building your knowledge

Discuss the quotation from Sam Selvon on page 126 of the Student Book, which further contextualises the writer's intent, and the influence this has on the language techniques used to create effect. Direct students towards the Key terms box and ensure they understand the meanings of the language techniques mentioned. Activity 5c could be undertaken as a class if students find this challenging, with teachers leading on the first sentence (I do), and students contributing for the second (you do).

Activity 6 Putting it all together

Students can use the bullet list of techniques on page 126 and table on dialect features on page 125 to co-create success criteria for the task ahead. Drama and discussion provide students with opportunities to share ideas prior to Activity 6b. Students could imagine themselves in a particular place and create still images or a 30-second scene to explore their own feelings and generate ideas to use in their writing. Modelling is important here; the example in the Student Book offers scope for teacher instruction. Students could then write their own paragraph and share this with a partner for peer assessment using the success criteria.

Additional activities

As homework, students could collect examples of dialect and accent from their own environment by talking to older people about how others have viewed the way that they talk.

To extend students' knowledge of synonyms, provide students with two words that are synonyms but are used in different contexts and ask them to decide which is most appropriate in a selection of sentence examples. In the context of this unit, and literature more broadly, 'melancholy' could be considered alongside 'sad'.

Unit focus

Objectives

Students will:

- learn how a poet conveys the power of a natural landscape
- explore how poetic structure and imagery are used to create mood
- analyse a poem for what it reveals about the poet's attitude to nature.

Unit texts

- ◁)) 'Written near a port on a dark evening' Charlotte Smith
- **k** 'Composed upon Westminster Bridge, September 3, 1802' William Wordsworth **WS**

Assessment

k 3.3 Mini-checkpoint quiz

Key terms

- **archaic** old-fashioned, from a different historical time
- **iambic pentameter** a line of poetry with five iambic 'feet'. An iambic foot is a pair of syllables: one unstressed syllable followed by a stressed one (as in 'da DUM')
- **imagery** language that creates pictures in the reader's mind
- **personification** showing something non-human as having human characteristics
- **prose** written language in its ordinary form, rather than poetry or drama
- **quatrain** a stanza of four lines, often with a strict rhythm and rhyme scheme
- **rhyming couplet** two consecutive lines of poetry that have rhyming final words
- **Romantic era** a cultural movement in the late 18th and early 19th centuries, which emphasised intense emotion and idealised the natural world
- **sonnet** a short poetic form, typically of 14 lines with ten syllables per line

Introduction to the unit

Unit 3.3 *How do poets present the power of nature?* is an opportunity for students to analyse structure and imagery in poetry, and to understand how writers use these techniques to create mood. Students will be introduced to new and potentially challenging concepts of poetic form through the study of the key text, Charlotte Smith's sonnet 'Written near a port on a dark evening'. Smith's poetry reflects the Romantic ideals of her contemporaries Wordsworth and Shelley and contains similar motifs, such as brooding natural imagery. This therefore offers students an opportunity to build on the work completed on Lamb and Wordsworth in Unit 3.1 and the exploration of feelings about nature and the subsequent mood a writer creates.

Activities

Starter activity

The sonnet draws links between sound and mood. Students could discuss how sounds can create different moods, drawing on their own experiences of natural or urban, mechanical, industrial or musical sounds.

⚙ Activity 1

Some students will be able to draw on first-hand experiences of the coast; others will need visual and auditory prompts, such as physical artefacts (shells, fossils) or examples from film and literature. Discuss the symbolism and purpose of beaches and how these intertwine. Historically, beaches have been scenes of major and catastrophic battles, but they are also

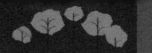

used in literature as sites of uncertainty, magic or conflict. The image in the Student Book provides a further prompt which can be scaffolded using the given vocabulary.

Ⓚ Kerboodle

The following activities can be replaced by the text and activities on 3.3 'Composed upon Westminster Bridge' worksheet.

Activity 2 Boosting your vocabulary

Ask students to use the context of the words in the poem to help them to work out their meanings. Which of the words would they use today with a different meaning? Consider exploring related words (e.g. 'embark', 'disembark', 'barge').

Activity 3 Building your knowledge

Before starting this activity, ask students what they already know about the sonnet form, perhaps from Year 7 or KS2. To scaffold for students, pre-select quotations from the poem for students to match to the relevant section. To extend, differentiate between Shakespearean and Petrarchan sonnets. Smith's is an example of the former, while the latter is structured in two sections: an octet (eight lines) followed by a sestet (six lines). This supports their understanding for Activity 6, in which students will consider how the poem's structure helps to convey its meaning.

Activity 4 Building your knowledge

Students can develop their understanding of the poem's language by exploring the contrasts in imagery. Confirm students' understanding of what imagery is before beginning these tasks. For students who need support, it would be helpful to point out particular lines and ask them to identify what type of contrast is being drawn in each example (e.g. 'black shadow/lucid line': dark and light). To help exploration of ideas about height and depth, pairs of students could track through the poem and find words which relate to movement or position, such as 'above' and 'o'er'. More confident students could explore the bigger ideas of the poem, such as how contrasting imagery reflects the poet's own feelings of uncertainty; 'fairy fires', for example, being a symbol of inconstancy.

Activity 5 Building your knowledge

Students examine how Smith uses language to create a particular mood. During the reading of the poem, draw attention to her use of contrast between sound and silence, her use of personification to animate the landscape, and the sense of isolation felt by the distant human figures. The given vocabulary will help students articulate their responses with more subtlety which they can then use with confidence in their analysis in Activity 6.

⚙ Activity 6 Putting it all together

This synoptic activity asks students to critically asses how the poet's structural and language choices create a certain mood. The sentence starters provided could form the basis of a class discussion, with students put into two groups and asked to present their arguments – this is a great opportunity to draw on the skills students have learned in argument and debate from Chapter 1. Use the example in Activity 5 to generate success criteria for making well-developed points.

⚙ Stretch yourself

This activity draws attention to Smith's exclusion from the Romantic canon. This provides an opportunity to discuss the 'canon', who decides it, what qualifications or characteristics are needed to be included (including gender and race), and whether it is something to be questioned. Students might decide on their own cultural 'canon' based on their own interests. Set up consensus circle activities to enable each student to argue their case for a text's inclusion.

Additional activities

Create a choral reading of the poem: add sound effects to enhance its atmosphere.

As a challenge, take the opportunity to introduce a pared-down version of the idea that nature, to the Romantic poets, is an overwhelming force. Students might think of the thrill of seeing a lightning storm or the sense of awe when standing on a clifftop. Ask: *How does Smith convey the awesome power of nature in this poem?*

Students could write a prose version, adopting different perspectives such as that of the sailor.

Unit focus

Objectives

Students will:

- learn how writers use setting to create narrative tension
- explore how narrative perspective, foreshadowing and sensory description help to build tension
- write the opening of a story, using descriptions of the setting to build tension.

Unit texts

- ◁» *An Emotion of Great Delight* Tahereh Mafi
- Ⓚ *Anita and Me* Meera Syal **WS**

Assessment

Ⓚ 3.4 Mini-checkpoint quiz; Chapter 3 Checkpoint 1 reading assessment; Chapter 3 Checkpoint 1 writing assessment

Key terms

- **first-person narrative** a story told by someone as if they were involved in the events themselves, using first-person pronouns, e.g. *I* and *we*
- **foreshadowing** a technique that gives a hint of something that will develop later
- **symbol** something specific that represents a more general quality or situation
- **tension** a feeling of being on edge with nerves stretched tight

Introduction to the unit

Unit 3.4 *How is setting used to create tension?* uses students' prior knowledge of structure, mood and style to inform their reading of the extract taken from the opening of Tahereh Mafi's novel *An Emotion of Great Delight*. The extract is unconventional in its description of place, prioritising initially the senses of touch and taste. The suffocating mood of the text is reinforced by the narrator's feelings of confinement. The subsequent activities draw out these learning points: students will explore mood and structure, and consider the writer's use of place, symbolism and narrative voice. Students will then use this knowledge to write their own description of a place using similar techniques to Mafi.

The events in the extract take place in America in 2003 and describe the experiences of a young Muslim as she attempts to negotiate a post-9/11 world. Teachers may need to provide additional background knowledge about 9/11 but this should be done in a sensitive way as it may be a difficult topic for students. The police officer's actions in the extract are representative of society's increasing levels of paranoia and prejudice towards the Muslim community in the aftermath of the terrorist attacks, with the narrator's backpack becoming a symbol of this paranoia. The narrator's fear and anger, expressed at the end of the extract, are therefore more comprehensible given this information.

Activities

Starter activity

An important element of this unit is thinking about description that prioritises senses other than sight. In fiction, sight and sound can often dominate, so encourage students to explore the other senses in creative ways, e.g. students could be shown images and be directed to describe them using each of the senses in turn. Modify this activity based on any individual needs of students.

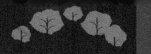

 Activity 1

This activity is a pre-reading prediction task. Remind students of their work on setting in Unit 3.1. The quotations hint at the text's focus on senses other than sight. The quotations permit a range of interpretations: the narrator might be in a rural or an urban place; emotions are ambiguous – there is a sense of freedom and of restraint; there is a sensation of warmth that is both refreshing and oppressive; there is noise and there is silence. Students might suggest that the narrator is on holiday, suggested by familiar iconography such as airplanes and sunshine.

🄚 Kerboodle

The following activities can be replaced by the text and activities on 3.4 *Anita and Me* worksheet.

Activity 2 Boosting your vocabulary

Students could produce Frayer models of the given words or use them in new sentences. Students should also consider the importance of these words in the context of the extract.

Activity 3 Building your knowledge

Students have the chance to check their predictions from Activity 1. The contrast between external movement and the narrator's sense of stasis is stark, as is her desire to escape her environment. Her decision to lie on the asphalt (tarmac) reflects her 'oncoming hysteria': it suggests an unconventional narrator, but it also connects her physically and inextricably with the landscape – as if she wants to disappear into it. Asking students why the narrator might want to disappear, to be invisible, would help them connect this section to the second half of the extract which introduces the police officer and the sense of sight.

Activity 4 Building your knowledge

In this activity students will undertake a writing task focusing on the senses to describe setting. Prepare students for writing with one of the following activities, adapting them for the individual needs of students:

- Look at photographs of places and ask students to think about how the place might be described through the other senses.

- Listen closely to audio recordings of different environments (rural and urban) and consider the various sounds to be heard. Provide students with relevant tier 2 vocabulary to help them offer more sophisticated responses.

- Give students different artefacts. They should then write a description of the object using the senses of touch, smell and sound where relevant. Students can then share this description with another student who will need to guess what they are describing.

Activity 5 Building your knowledge

Begin by displaying images that convey impressions of heat (objects, people, landscapes) and discuss their connotations. Alternatively, look at idiomatic expressions (such as song titles) and discuss what impressions they convey: 'if you can't stand the heat, get out of the kitchen'; 'the heat of the moment'. Explore the links between the weather and pressure; how do we respond to pressure as people?

Activity 6 Building your knowledge

This activity discusses foreshadowing and symbolism as literary devices, which some students may need introducing to. It might help to model how a writer would plan foreshadowing and incorporate it throughout a piece of writing.

Activity 7 Putting it all together

Ask students to consider their responses to Activity 4 when planning their writing. The Kerboodle resource *Preparing for writing* may be useful here. To begin, teachers could use the example response as a model to deconstruct how the author has used language and structure, highlighting the examples as a guide. For less confident students, encourage them to use a familiar context and use the structure of the example as a model.

Stretch yourself

This activity gives students the opportunity to engage critically with the text. The statement could form the basis of discussion, with students offering textual detail to support their reasons.

Additional activities

Ask students to rewrite parts of the extract from *An Emotion of Great Delight*, or other texts, using different narrative perspectives. They could then discuss the effects created and what the revised version adds to, or loses from, the original.

Unit focus

Objectives

Students will:

- learn how writers actively influence the reader's attitude towards place
- explore how juxtaposition, descriptive detail and language choices build up a sense of place
- comment on how a writer influences the reader's attitude towards a place.

Unit texts

- ◁» *The Unofficial Countryside* Richard Mabey
- 𝕜 'A Walk on the Wild Side' Sarah Gardner **WS**

Assessment

𝕜 3.5 Mini-checkpoint quiz

Key terms

- **infer** to work something out from what is seen, said or done, even though it is not stated directly
- **juxtapose** to put words, ideas or images together to show a contrast or relationship between them
- **metaphor** a comparison that says one thing is something else, e.g. *Amy was a rock*

Introduction to the unit

Unit 3.5 *How do writers make ordinary places interesting?* marks a change in chapter focus from fictional and/or literary interpretations of place, to how writers describe the shifting landscape and engage creatively and rhetorically with current ecological and environmental concerns. The extract from Richard Mabey's *The Unofficial Countryside*, written in the 1970s, deals with the overlap between the built and the natural environments. He finds something to celebrate in these wasteland and derelict areas – often referred to as 'edgelands' – and this genre of nature writing has become popular in recent years. Edgelands are full of contradictions: to some, they are ugly blots on the landscape; to others they provide evidence of nature's resilience. This unit challenges students' perspectives on edgeland space but also gives them the vocabulary to respond articulately to the ideas presented.

Activities

Starter activity

This unit, and indeed the whole chapter, celebrates the diversity of place and challenges students' preconceptions. Their experiences of both familiar and unfamiliar places can be explored by asking them to bring in photographs of their own favourite locations. They could then act as travel guides and try to persuade others to pay a visit by using only positive language.

⚙ Activity 1

The image used for Activity 1 encapsulates the ideas in this unit. Draw attention to the contrast of the industrial and natural or the flowing water and brick buildings. Activity 1b ties the image to previous work on setting and genre in Units 3.1–3.4. Students could be encouraged to refer to TV and film to support and enhance their ideas. This might be an opportunity to revisit the iconography of space and genre, first explored in the chapter opener. For Activity 1c,

teachers could ask students to think of how different people might describe the image: a builder, a crime prevention officer, a conservationist, etc.

Kerboodle

The following activities can be replaced by the text and activities on 3.5 'A Walk on the Wild Side' worksheet.

Activity 2 Boosting your vocabulary

Introduce students to animal imagery by showing them photographs and discussing the characteristics and associations of each animal, such as a horse for nobility, war, sport; a bee for summer, or connotations of busyness; snakes for slyness and cunning. To support in Activity 2b, provide sentences and ask students to fill in the blank with the correct words.

Activity 3 Building your knowledge

Teachers can use the information in the teaching text above the activity to prepare for this activity, which requires students to examine the structure of the text. Make explicit the idea that structure is another way of thinking about how a writer takes us on a journey through the text. One way of reading the text visually to follow its structure, or path, is to storyboard the sequence and annotate it with relevant quotations. This will prepare students for the next activity, which requires them to explore the language of the text.

Activity 4 Building your knowledge

On the journey, Mabey transports the reader from the built urban environment to the patch of natural land by the river, and the language he uses to describe the places becomes progressively more positive. Teachers could draw attention to this by asking students to identify quotations and put them on a positive–negative continuum. Students could then reflect on how Mabey persuades us to his point of view. For Activity 4b, teachers will need to be sensitive to their students' context. Mabey's perspective on the housing estate might be more influenced by his love of nature and disdain for the built environment, rather than a negative opinion on housing estates and the residents themselves. However, the phrase 'living factory' is worth spending some time over. It is important that teachers use this unit to explore how readers can be influenced by a writer's perspective and why it is important to also question that perspective. Links could be made to the exploration of opinion students engaged with in Unit 1.6, when they considered the ways the press try to influence their readers. Ask: *What similarities are there between the techniques Mabey uses to present his point of view and the way a newspaper editorial might present the journalist's view?*

Activity 5 Building your knowledge

The statements provided could form the basis of a discussion. One way of organising this in the classroom is to use a fishbowl-discussion technique: two students discuss one of the statements, observed by another pair who look for how the discussion develops, then switch roles. Teachers could provide success criteria such as 'Quality of talk' (Who takes the lead? Who builds and develops points? Who is more assertive? Do the speakers use complete sentences in their talk?) and 'Quality of content' (Do the speakers refer to textual detail to support their points? Do the speakers refer to particular linguistic techniques?).

Activity 6 Putting it all together

Activity 5 can be used as a springboard for this activity. It may be helpful for students to review their answers to Activity 5, using this to co-create success criteria for use while planning and writing in Activity 6. For less confident students, provide sentence starters for each step in the Student Book. To extend, ask students to find further language devices to support their answers, outside of those covered in this unit.

Additional activities

To support some of the ideas in the Student Book and Kerboodle activities, teachers could read the description of the marshland in Dickens' *Great Expectations* or Clive King's *Stig of the Dump* which contain effective descriptions of wasteland locations. Pose critical statements to students for discussion, as in Activities 5 and 6.

Unit focus

Objectives

Students will:

- learn how a writer uses shifting landscapes to create contrasting moods
- explore how writers borrow styles from other genres
- write about a place, creating contrasting moods.

Unit texts

- ◁» *The Easternmost House* Juliet Blaxland
- 𝕜 *The Feast* Margaret Kennedy **WS**

Assessment

𝕜 3.6 Mini-checkpoint quiz

Key terms

- **antonym** a word that has the opposite meaning of a particular word
- **connotation** an idea or feeling linked to a word, as well as its main meaning
- **convention** a typical feature you find in a particular genre
- **genre** a type of story, e.g. *horror, romance, adventure, science fiction*
- **intertextuality** the links (direct or indirect) between individual texts

Introduction to the unit

Unit 3.6 *How are shifting landscapes presented?* returns to coastal settings, building on the work in Unit 3.3. Whereas Unit 3.5 examined the liminal spaces between country and city, Blaxland's text is a powerful and atmospheric account of the conflict between sea and land, providing several exciting opportunities for discussion and textual interrogation. On one level, Blaxland explores the impact of soil erosion on coastal areas, thus introducing an environmental theme and useful links to Geography. However, Blaxland's style is rich with allusion and intertextuality, creating an uncanny mood through the language of ghost and horror stories. The Did you know? fact helps broaden students' literary capital: teachers can use this to explore the work of M. R. James. Teachers can also draw on the activities from the chapter opener which explore attitudes to a number of locations, including an image of a coastal town.

Activities

Starter activity

The unit introduces students to intertextuality. This is a difficult concept: begin by displaying a few examples and discussing the impact of these, so that students have a full understanding of the term before embarking on the activities in the unit.

⚙ Activity 1

Students have already considered mood in Units 3.2–3.4. In this chapter, mood is treated as a writer's technique and so mood and atmosphere are interchangeable concepts. Film is an excellent way to explore mood: the combination of image and sound (and editing) provides students with a recognisable 'language' to discuss mood. Discuss contemporary and familiar texts to engage students. Graphic novels and their highly stylised use of images could also provide exciting stimuli.

(k) Kerboodle

The following activities can be replaced by the text and activities on 3.6 *The Feast* worksheet.

Activity 2 Boosting your vocabulary

The Frayer model is a helpful technique to explore words in more detail and this strategy can be used to examine other words in the text. Students could select further words to explore. In Activity 2c remind students of how the use of the word 'unromantic' might be different from the concept of 'Romanticism' introduced in Unit 3.3.

Activity 3 Building your knowledge

Looking at bygone photographs of the local area to consider how the landscape has changed might be a useful strategy to introduce students to the bigger ideas in this unit. Here, students examine the contrasts in the text and Activity 3c can be used to stimulate interesting class discussion. Students could use a pyramid template to create a hierarchy (three at the bottom, two in the middle, one at the top), with students taking one of their choices and justifying its importance to the rest of the group. Teachers could introduce the ideas explored in Activity 3d by asking the class to think about aspects of their own home they might miss in Blaxland's place – whether an object or a feeling.

⚙ Activity 4 Building your knowledge

Teachers could provide a range of different text genres and explore their conventions; students can draw on their learning of genre and convention from Chapter 2. Openings to stories and films that are familiar to students are particularly useful, such as *Stranger Things* and *ET*, as they will provide students with recognisable moving image contexts in which to look at similarities of characterisation, setting and plot.

Activity 5 Building your knowledge

Activity 5 looks closely at ghost story conventions and how Blaxland uses them. Encourage students' confidence and knowledge arising from what they have learned in Units 2.1 and 2.4. Ensure students understand the word 'impending' and how it links to suspense and tension. Explore how this relates to events that are yet to happen, and how this might be expressed with the use of future tenses. Students could discuss in pairs before writing their response

to Activity 5b. To extend learning of intertextuality, students could explore how Tom Becker's *Darkside* combines Dickensian London and contemporary horror.

Activity 6 Putting it all together

In this activity, students use the knowledge of mood and atmosphere learned during this unit to write a creative description. In preparation for this, teachers could show images of a place at two different times or time-lapse footage of a city; or students could bring photographs of their own to stimulate discussion. Working with students on the trigger for the shift in mood will also help deepen their understanding of narrative structure.

⚙ Stretch yourself

This activity draws together work on structure but places the focus on the use of space and mood as a structural device, rather than solely focusing on chronology. It may be helpful to suggest that students think of the text in cinematic terms, and visualise how the focus would shift throughout the scene to depict the written details.

Additional activities

Students could create an audio reading of the extract, using voice and sound effects to create mood.

Following on from Activity 3, students could find postcards or take photographs of their area. They could then write to their future selves, describing their feelings about the place, what they think might change and what they would miss if it were to disappear.

Teachers could introduce further reading texts to enhance students' literary knowledge and make comparisons with Blaxland's text. For example, Susan Hill's atmospheric descriptions of the coastal setting in *The Woman in Black*; graphic novels (e.g. *Batman*: *Gothic*) and fine art (e.g. Edward Hopper's paintings) which students can annotate to explore the visual conventions used by artists to convey mood. Seamus Heaney's 'Storm on the Island' also uses dramatic and eerie language to describe the power of nature in a place.

3.7 How can we write about environmental issues?

Unit focus

Objectives

Students will:

- learn more about rhetorical skills
- explore how to structure and present an argument
- write and present their point of view about an environmental issue.

Unit texts

- 🔊 'Taking our future into our own hands' Dr Mya-Rose Craig
- 🅚 Severn Cullis-Suzuki's speech, 1992 **WS**

Assessment

🅚 3.7 Mini-checkpoint quiz

Key terms

- **fluency** speaking with a smooth flow, without hesitating
- **gesture** using your hands to indicate meaning, e.g. to help emphasise certain points
- **pace** the speed at which someone speaks or moves or something happens
- **persuasive** making you want to do or believe something
- **rhetorical device** a language feature that has a persuasive or impressive effect on listeners and readers

Introduction to the unit

Unit 3.7 *How can we write about environmental issues?* develops the theme of changing landscapes explored in Units 3.5 and 3.6 but also widens the object of study by considering the impact of human behaviour on the global environment. The text is written by an influential young environmentalist Dr Mya-Rose Craig, and refers to the Youth Strikes for Climate movement inspired by Greta Thunberg (Unit 1.2), but is structured following the approach of the classical political writer Cicero. By considering the political power of rhetoric, students can learn about the power of human agency and perhaps consider the obstacles to change. Unit 3.7 continues the study of structure and looks forward to further study of rhetoric and persuasion in Quest 3 Chapter 1 *Truth and reality*. The final activity asks students to write and deliver a speech: this can be challenging for some and so teachers will need to think about how these speeches might be presented, e.g. students could use video or present to small groups.

Activities

⚙ Starter activity

Show some recent news clips on climate change to gauge students' understanding of the topic. Greta Thunberg is an obvious starting point and students should recognise her from their study in Unit 1.2. Invite students to share their opinions on climate change. Ask also why this particular topic has motivated young people more than any other group of people.

⚙ Activity 1

Activate students' prior learning by asking them to think about different forms of persuasive writing (e.g. travel brochures, leaflets, advertisements).
As explored in Unit 1.7, image selection reinforces the message in media texts and using impactful images is vital to the effect on a reader. Activity 1c and 1d require students to think deeply about these choices. Teachers could provide captions for each image to demonstrate how it is possible to interpret imagery

in different ways and change or subvert the meaning, e.g. two captions for the placards image could be: 'Young people fight for environmental action' and 'Crowds stop traffic during protest', each prompting a different response in the reader.

Ⓚ Kerboodle

The following activities can be replaced by the text and activities on 3.7 Severn Cullis-Suzuki's 1992 speech worksheet.

Activity 2 Boosting your vocabulary

Words such as 'disenfranchised' and 'plundering' are emotive and these, along with other words in the text such as 'lobbying', introduce students to the language of politics. 'Plundering' has connotations of Viking invasions, and an awareness of this can help deepen students' understanding of why this word has such impact.

Activity 3 Building your knowledge

This section is important in building students' understanding of the structure of a speech. As with all structures, this is not completely fixed and teachers should make it clear that writers manipulate structure for effect. The table in Activity 3 helpfully matches the structural elements to the phase of Craig's argument, and provides a good opportunity for students to practise scanning texts and identifying evidence independently. To support less confident students, teachers could provide further examples from the text and/or explanations for students to make the connections.

Activity 4 Building your knowledge

Activity 4 shifts the focus to spoken language in preparation for the final synoptic activity. Prepare students for this section by showing them video footage of other speakers (e.g. politicians and celebrities) and looking at the physical aspects of talk – how speakers use some of the features shown in the diagram to engage their audience. Activity 4 requires students to become 'speech directors' by offering advice to a speaker on their delivery. Ask students to make notes on the selected section of the speech using the prompts given. Students may find it helpful (and engaging) to test out their ideas aloud, by sharing their notes with a partner for them to follow, so they can check whether the instructions they have given produce the intended effects, then making adjustments where necessary.

Activity 5 Building your knowledge

Students deliver four small sections of the speech, a task which is less intimidating and gives them the opportunity to practise speaking aloud ahead of writing and delivering their own speech. Students could work in small groups, trying out the different moods and tones, and emphasising different words. They could also offer feedback to each other using the 'presentation skills' diagram on page 156 of the Student Book.

Activity 6 Putting it all together

The Student Book provides two provocative statements, but teachers could consider other topics. It is important that students research their chosen topic beforehand so that there is substance behind the style. Allow students to do a couple of drafts with teacher feedback to promote confidence, while also giving an opportunity to practise presenting sections to a small audience. As mentioned in the introduction to this unit, the final speech can be delivered in a range of contexts, including students filming themselves and sharing this on a school platform. To extend this activity, host a speaking competition or set up a Q&A session at the end of some of the speeches.

Additional activities

Teachers could talk about the influence that classical texts still have over contemporary culture, such as in Maths, Physics, English and Classics. Students could collect examples from classical literature that they are familiar with, such as those from Greek mythology. Contemporary children's and Young Adult literature draw heavily on classical texts, e.g. *The Hunger Games* (Suzanne Collins), *Artemis Fowl* (Eoin Colfer) and *Percy Jackson* (Rick Riordan), to name but a few.

Stretch students further by asking them to consider a number of counter-arguments that Craig could have included in Section 5 of her argument, e.g. 'Some people might say that climate change is inevitable'. Students could take one of these statements and write a new section of the article providing a suitable counter-argument.

Unit focus

Objectives

Students will:

- learn about the subgenre of climate fiction
- understand what is meant by exposition in a narrative
- consider the ways in which a writer presents future worlds.

Unit texts

- ◁» *Exodus* Julie Bertagna
- Ⓚ *Memory of Water* Emmi Itäranta **WS**

Assessment

Ⓚ 3.8 Mini-checkpoint quiz; Chapter 3 Checkpoint 2 reading assessment; Chapter 3 Checkpoint 2 writing assessment

Key terms

- **exposition** (in a story) background information, often giving details about what happened before the story began
- **inference** a conclusion reached by reasoning
- **neologism** a newly created word or expression, or a new meaning for an existing word
- **subgenre** a subdivision of a genre, e.g. climate fiction is a subgenre of science fiction

Introduction to the unit

Unit 3.8 *How do writers describe future spaces?* provides a logical conclusion to Chapter 3. Thus far, students have considered how writers use real and imagined settings to produce different emotions, from elation to alienation. They have also learned how the landscape is mutable, subject to the destructive forces brought about by human action. Julie Bertagna's *Exodus*, from which this unit's text is taken, confronts the consequences of human behaviour in a world where rising sea levels have impacted significantly on the human population. *Exodus* is an example of climate fiction, a subgenre of science fiction. In many ways, it anticipates the dystopian narratives covered in Quest 3 Chapter 2 *Utopia and dystopia*, but climate fiction can be considered in its own right as a genre which explores the impact of environmental catastrophe upon human life rather than dystopian tropes such as authoritarian politics, destructive and divisive ideologies, and errant technology.

Activities

✿ Starter activity

Start by showing some images of science fiction landscapes and ask students how these are different from the places they have looked at thus far in the chapter. Show some dramatic images of real places that are affected by climate change (e.g. through fire, drought, flooding) and ask how students might feel if this were commonplace. Be sensitive to climate hardship students may have endured.

✿ Activity 1

Science fiction will be a recognisable genre to students. Point out that science fiction is not a new genre and that Mary Shelley's *Frankenstein* (1818) is considered to be one of the oldest science fiction novels in English. Activity 1b introduces the idea that future worlds are often based on contemporary concerns. Students may view the different scenarios as positive or negative. Encourage discussion around the four topics.

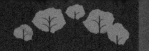

Ⓚ Kerboodle

The following activities can be replaced by the text and activities on 3.8 *Memory of Water* Emmi Itäranta worksheet.

Activity 2 Boosting your vocabulary

This activity includes work on the term 'neologism' which is very relevant when reading about future worlds. Emphasise that neologisms are introduced all the time. Provide students with more examples (e.g. 'biopic', 'cyberspace'), and invite them to suggest others. Ask students to explore when one or two were first used and discuss the context in which they were created.

Activity 3 Building your knowledge

The Building your knowledge section is important for its explanation of climate fiction as a subgenre of science fiction. Ensure students understand the term 'subgenre', before explaining the differences between climate fiction and more familiar forms of science fiction. In climate fiction, the future world described is entirely credible, contains recognisable characteristics of life today, and a current environmental issue forms the basis of the narrative. Characters cannot change the world – the environmental damage is irreversible – and the emphasis is upon how characters deal with this reality. In contrast, traditional science fiction uses scenarios that we might not have considered yet, and characters might be able to alter their future (e.g. in films such as *Meet the Robinsons*, *Ender's Game* or *Avengers: Endgame*). Activity 3 reinforces knowledge of climate fiction conventions by looking at familiar and unfamiliar elements of the world in the text. Draw attention to the references to the church and standing stones in the extract. Ask: *What might these tell us about this future community?* To support less confident students, provide quotations from the text to be fitted into the table.

Activity 4 Building your knowledge

To support students' understanding of exposition, gather examples from other texts or explore the concept in class readers. The author Stephen King suggested that while every character has a back story or history, most of that won't be interesting. Good writers stick to writing about the parts that are interesting. Students could consider this when looking at the two examples. After completing Activity 4, ask students: *What did you learn from this activity about how to improve your own writing?*

Activity 5 Building your knowledge

Start by exploring what inference is by using images, and ask students to discuss what they understand about place or people from the images (for example, a photograph of a snowy landscape leads us to infer that it is cold). Students could write a sentence about a cold place without using the word 'cold' (or its synonyms) to help them see how this can be an effective form of storytelling.

Activity 6 Putting it all together

Teachers can scaffold this activity through group discussion. For each of the bullet points, students could find evidence from the text and explain why it is important. For less confident students, teachers could provide relevant quotations as well as, for more confident students, a few red herrings to invite debate.

Stretch yourself

The inclusion of relics in science fiction helps to build recognisable worlds. Showing students images from films, such as the Statue of Liberty at the end of *Planet of the Apes* (1968), may be helpful. This also presents an opportunity to discuss cross-curricular links to History and Archaeology and the significance of these objects or landmarks to our understanding of the world and past civilisations. It could be a nostalgic reminder of what we have lost (see also Unit 3.6), or even more controversially it could be that the inclusion of relics highlights our obsession with artefacts and material things (see Additional activities below).

Additional activities

Some critics have said that the inclusion of relics in science-fiction stories reveals how much humans value 'things'. To what extent do students agree?

Consolidate students' learning with the following chapter-reflective questions:

- *Which of these units has been most effective in changing the way that you think about a place?*

- *Which of the extracts was most successful in evoking a sense of place?*

- *Look back at the images from the chapter opener. Has this chapter changed how you feel about these places?*

Encourage students to comment on structure and language techniques, and support with quotations.

Quest key terms glossary

abbreviation a shortened form of a word or phrase

ambiguity having more than one meaning

anecdote a short or entertaining story about real people or events

antagonist main opponent

antithesis a rhetorical device that expresses opposing or contrasting ideas

antonym a word that has the opposite meaning of a particular word

archaic old-fashioned, from a different historical time

autobiography the story of a person's life, written by that person

biography the story of a person's life, written by someone else

chairperson a person who is in charge of a meeting

chronological order the order in which things happened

clause a part of a sentence with its own verb

colloquial suitable for ordinary conversation rather than formal speech or writing

colloquial language informal words or phrases that are suitable for ordinary conversation, rather than formal speech or writing

complex sentence a multi-clause sentence with at least one subordinate clause, e.g. *He stopped because he was tired.*

connotation an idea or feeling linked to a word, as well as its main meaning

context the time, place and influences on a text from when it was written, and from when it is read, which shape our understanding of the text

convention a typical feature you find in a particular genre

counter-argument an argument that opposes the point put forward

declarative a sentence that makes a statement

dialect a form of a language linked to a specific region, e.g. Geordie in Newcastle upon Tyne

direct address addressing the reader as you

direct speech the words that are actually spoken, usually presented in quotation marks

discourse marker a word or phrase that makes a link between points and organises text

editorial a newspaper article expressing a writer's opinion

emotive language word choices that create a strong emotional reaction in the audience or reader

epigram the expression of an idea in a short, memorable way

etymology a description of the origin and history of a particular word

exclamatory statement a sentence that expresses sudden or strong emotions, such as excitement. It usually ends with an exclamation mark

exposition (in a story) background information, often giving details about what happened before the story began

extended metaphor a long metaphor which builds up an image in detail over many lines

figurative language words or phrases with a meaning that is different from the literal meaning

first-person narrative a story told by someone as if they were involved in the events themselves, using first-person pronouns, e.g. *I* and *we*

fluency speaking with a smooth flow, without hesitating

foreshadowing a technique that gives a hint of something that will develop later

genre a type of story, e.g. *horror, romance, adventure, science fiction*

gesture using your hands to indicate meaning, e.g. to help emphasise certain points

homophone a word that sounds the same as another, but is spelled differently and means something different

iambic pentameter a line of poetry with five iambic 'feet'. An iambic foot is a pair of syllables: one unstressed syllable followed by a stressed one (as in 'da DUM')

imagery language that creates pictures in the reader's mind

imperative a sentence that gives an order, command or instruction

infer to work something out from what is seen, said or done, even though it is not stated directly

inference a conclusion reached by reasoning

interrogative a sentence that asks a question

intertextuality the links (direct or indirect) between individual texts

juxtapose to put words, ideas or images together to show a contrast or relationship between them

metaphor a comparison that says one thing is something else, e.g. *Amy was a rock*

modal verb a verb that works with another verb to show that something needs to happen or might possibly happen, e.g. *must, shall, will, should, would, can, could, may* and *might*

motion a statement, idea or policy that is discussed in a debate

multi-clause sentence a sentence with more than one clause, each with its own main verb, e.g. *The judge frowned and lifted her hammer.*

multimodal having or involving many methods (modes), e.g. text, images, motion, audio

narrative voice the perspective (viewpoint) from which a story is told, and the style in which it is told

narrator a person who tells a story, especially in a book, play or film

neologism a newly created word or expression, or a new meaning for an existing word

non-standard English an informal version of English, often used with family and friends, including slang and regional variations

noun phrase a noun plus information before and/or after the noun

opposition a statement that opposes a judgement or opinion

pace the speed at which someone speaks or moves or something happens

past tense a verb form that shows actions or events that have already happened

personification showing something non-human as having human characteristics

persuasive making you want to do or believe something

possessive determiner a word that comes before a noun to show whose it is, e.g. *my, your, her*

prefix a word or group of letters placed in front of another word to add to or change its meaning

present tense a verb form that describes actions which are happening now

pronoun a word used instead of a noun or noun phrase, e.g. *he, it, they*

pronunciation the sound made when a word is spoken

proposition a statement that expresses a judgement or opinion

prose written language in its ordinary form, rather than poetry or drama

quatrain a stanza of four lines, often with a strict rhythm and rhyme scheme

recount an account (written or spoken) of an event or experience

register the manner of speaking or writing, which can range between formal and informal

repetition using the same word or phrase more than once

rhetorical device a language feature that has a persuasive or impressive effect on listeners and readers

rhetorical question a question asked for dramatic effect and not intended to get an answer

rhyme using the same sound to end words, particularly at the ends of lines

rhyming couplet two consecutive lines of poetry that have rhyming final words

rhythm the pattern of beats in a line of music or poetry

Romantic era a cultural movement in the late 18th and early 19th centuries, which emphasised intense emotion and idealised the natural world

root the core of a word that has meaning. It may or may not be a complete word

sarcasm the use of humour or saying the opposite of what is meant to mock or criticise someone

second person a narrative voice that addresses the reader directly, using the pronoun *you*

setting where the action takes place

simile a comparison of one thing to another, using 'as' or 'like', e.g. *He swam like a fish*

slogan a short, catchy word or phrase used to advertise something or represent the aims of a campaign or organisation

sonnet a short poetic form, typically of 14 lines with ten syllables per line

Standard English a widely recognised formal version of English, not linked to any region, but used in schools, exams, official publications and in public announcements

subgenre a subdivision of a genre, e.g. climate fiction is a subgenre of science fiction

subvert to change an established way something is done

summarise to give the key points

superlative the form of an adjective or adverb that means 'most'

suspense a feeling of anxious uncertainty while waiting for something to happen or become known

symbol something specific that represents a more general quality or situation

synonym a word or phrase that means the same, or almost the same, as another word or phrase

tension a feeling of being on edge with nerves stretched tight

the floor the formal term to describe everyone participating in a debate apart from the chairperson and main speakers

the media all means of communicating with a large audience through various outlets, such as television broadcasting, advertising, newspapers and the Internet

the supernatural events and forces that cannot be explained by the known laws of nature or science

third person a narrative voice that informs the reader of what is taking place, using the pronouns *he, she* or *they*

This house believes… a formal way of introducing a motion

tone the speaker's or writer's feeling or attitude expressed towards their subject

tricolon a pattern of three words or phrases grouped together to be memorable and have impact

OXFORD
UNIVERSITY PRESS

Great Clarendon Street, Oxford, OX2 6DP, United Kingdom

Oxford University Press is a department of the University of Oxford.
It furthers the University's objective of excellence in research,
scholarship, and education by publishing worldwide. Oxford is a
registered trade mark of Oxford University Press in the UK and in
certain other countries.

Authors: Sarah Eggleton and Lance Hanson

First published in 2023

British Library Cataloguing in Publication Data
Data available

978-1-38-2033336

978-1-38-2033343

10 9 8 7 6 5 4 3 2 1

The manufacturing process conforms to the environmental regulations
of the country of origin.

Printed in Great Britain by CPI Group (UK) Ltd., Croydon CR0 4YY

Acknowledgements
The publisher and authors would like to thank the following for
permission to use copyright material:

Artwork by Michael Driver.

Every effort has been made to contact copyright holders of material
reproduced in this book. Any omissions will be rectified in subsequent
printings if notice is given to the publisher.